HOME MEMORIES.

HOME MEMORIES,

AND

RECOLLECTIONS OF A LIFE;

BY

BEN BRIERLEY,

AUTHOR OF "TALES AND SKETCHES OF LANCASHIRE LIFE," &C.

" The short and simple annals of the poor."

GRAY.

DEDICATED

TO THE SHARER OF MY HAPPINESS, SORROW, AND AFFLICTION,

MY WIFE.

CONTENTS.

viii. CONTENTS.

HOME MEMORIES.

AN AUTOBIOGRAPHICAL SKETCH.

I was born in the "Rocks." Do not imagine from this, dear reader, that my earliest home was among the mountains. There is nothing so wild and romantic attached to the place of my nativity. The humble tenement in which I first saw what should have been light, is situated in a hole caused by the raising of the road, so as to be on a level with the bridge that spans the Rochdale canal at Failsworth. This hole, called the "Rocks," from its being walled with stone, is wedge-shaped; and I was placed at the thin end. The upper portion of the house has since been rebuilt; and now forms a dwelling of itself, the lower part, in which I groped my way when I began to toddle and go into mischief, now serving only as a foundation. In the original plan of the building there was a door communicating with the principal bed-room and the road. This door served more purposes than one. Besides affording a means of escape when the basement was flooded, as was often the case, it was a convenience for drunken people to use their clogs against. Many a time have I listened to the music thus produced when wakened out of my childish dreams, as these serenades were more frequent than agreeable. The only peace we had was when my grandfather, who lived within a few doors, was constable.

My father, who was a handloom weaver, had been a soldier, but was discharged when very young, as the following record will attest: "His Majesty's Rocket Brigade of Royal Horse Artillery, whereof Lieut.-Colonel P. Tyers is Colonel. These are to certify that James Brierley, Gunner, in Major E. C. Whinyates' Rocket Troop in the Brigade aforesaid, born in the parish of Middleton, in or near the town of ————, in the county of Lancaster, was enlisted at the age of 17 years, and has served in the same Regiment for the space of 4 Years and 119 Days, as well as in other Corps, after the age of Eighteen, according to the following Statement, but in consequence of a Reduction is hereby discharged; having first received all just Demands of Pay, Clothing, &c., from his entry into the said Regiment, to the Date of his Discharge, as appears by his Receipt on the back hereof, and to prevent any improper use being made of this Discharge by its falling into other Hands, the following is a Description of the said James Brierley.—He is about 21 Years of Age, is 5 feet 7 inches in height, light hair, grey eyes, fresh complexion, by trade a weaver. STATEMENT OF SERVICE.—R. H. Artillery. From 2nd April, 1812, to July, 1816, 4 years, 119 days. Waterloo, 2 years. Total, 6 years, 119 days.*" This was beginning life, as a man, rather early; and singularly enough, he enlisted on his birthday. My grandfather used to say he ought to have been born a day earlier.

My father must have married soon after his return home, as before I was introduced to a station in life that was not of my seeking, there had been four other victims—two brothers, and two sisters. Fortunately they had but a short account to render to their Maker,—they died in their infancy. The immediate successor to the family cradle, your humble servant, began to suck his thumbs, so I have been informed, as I have no personal knowledge of the fact,—on the 26th of June, 1825. It was my mother's wish that I should have followed the youthful departed, as times were so bad that the look-out for rising progeny was of the most unpromising. But I cheated the sexton, as many children do who are felt to be in the way. My parents had to do the best they could with the little intruder, and help me to struggle to get a footing in the world. I have often thought that I owe as much to my mother's voice as I do to her love, for the charm of life which even poverty can sometimes experience. She had been a singer in the All Saints' Church choir at Newton Heath, the choir-master at the time being James Ridings, the father of the late Elijah of that "ilk." Her voice was a powerful contralto; and I can remember its clear mellow tones so far in the past as I can remember anything. I can hear them now. She was a gentle creature; and like the mother of "Malcolm" in "Macbeth," "died every day

---

* Being present at the Battle of Waterloo entitled him to an addition of 2 years to his service.

she lived." No woman of my acquaintance ever suffered more than she, or bore her sufferings with truer fortitude. But I speak now of her later life. It was her deep religious feeling that was her support in all her travails, and gave her cheerfulness when physical pain had her in its grip.

Before I was of a sufficient age to be sent to school I had a brother born. I did not give him the heartiest welcome, as I had fears that he might claim a joint possession of my spoon. I hated the sight of " Owd Jacky Wife " for bringing him into the world, and had serious thoughts of damaging her " parsley bed " by the introduction of cats. But " Little Tummy " grew into my liking as he grew more plump, and I allowed him to suck most of my farthing " humbug." I remember my first " breeching; " and my father taking me by the hand to walk all the way to Manchester, and stripped me in a shop in Sugar Lane, for a " try-on." I could not then have been more than four years old; but the suit of " bell-buttoned " velveteen in which my limbs had to look out themselves for a proper place in which to exercise, would have fitted a boy of ten. But I had to grow prodigiously, and the clothes had to do for my brother when I cast them off. Two maiden aunts who made a plaything of me, because of my being the oldest nephew, subscribed their pence, and endowed me with a hat; but a jealous uncle, not many years my senior, played a trick upon it that instead of its being used any longer as a covering for my head, I converted it into a substitute for a football. Previous to thus being attired I strutted about, with all the pride of a juvenile dandy, surrounded by the capacious folds of an old waistcoat belonging to my grandfather. My uncles gave me the nickname of " Owd Pee Collin," a man who worked on the road, because, like my prototype, I walked with my hands behind me, and would not have altered my pace if it had suddenly begun to rain " cats and dogs."

I could not have been more than four years old when it occurred to elder boys that they would have a rushcart. The " wakes " was near at hand; so preparations were begun at once. I do not remember how I got smuggled into the festive ranks, unless it was a condition of lending the wagon in which it was built, and I was quite a favourite with Aaron Andrew, the owner of it. In fact, I made his house one of my several homes; and his youngest daughter, who is still living, was more like a sister than a companion. I was not, however, permitted to be one of the " horses." I was too young to be either a " shafter " or a " leader;" so had to be content to be a " thrutcher " behind. It took two days to build the cart, the chief artificers in the work being the Thorley family, the since eminent musicians.

Whoever has taken part in the construction of this king of rustic pageants will remember with what anxiety the completion of the various stages are watched, especially when the supply of rushes falls short, and fresh raids have to be made on badly cultivated lands, and margins of old "pit-steads," for "short" rushes, and "bolts," the miles that have to be traversed before the much needed supply can be obtained, and the danger of encountering sore-minded farmers. Then above all, the sheet that is to adorn the front of the cart! How are we to muster ribbons to tie on the penny watches, and the various other trinkets, the loans of nurses, and the bouquets of flowers kindly furnished by the Booths, who are still noted flower growers? More than that, how were we to decorate ourselves out of a wardrobe seldom plentifully supplied? This latter difficulty I had no anxiety about, I knew that my aunts would see to this if they had to ransack all Failsworth for the material. Hat or cap I had none. The only one I had ever possessed I had made a football of, and my uncles had only one to serve the whole lot, so that could not be spared. But a much older boy—well, he was growing up into a young man—was prevailed upon to lend me his, a white "billy" it was, of no shape, except what it got from the last kicking, but with plenty of space for ventilation in what was by courtesy called the crown. Unfortunately for me the proper owner of the hat was not without a head, and by adding to its size a thick growth of bushy black hair that stood out like wire fringe, some idea may be formed of the kind of extinguisher I had to be placed beneath. But when it was covered with all colours and lengths of ribbons, and shreds of woven silk, it may be imagined that I appeared upon the scene a something of the nature of a variegated Skye terrier.

If I could have foreseen what the hat would have led to there would either have been a "thrutcher" less, or one would have been bareheaded. But I am anticipating events. It had rained heavily during the night preceding the wakes morning; but the morning itself was as fine as we were, overhead; but roads and lanes were not carpeted in those days, and seldom did the scraper go over them. The cart had been built at the bottom of a short road called the "Hottel," which after a night's rain would be well marked with the rings of pattens, and the indentions made by thickly soled clogs. The cart was ready for "drawing out;" the drummer was at his post, and had slung an old can over his shoulders with as much seriousness as if he had been appointed to lead up an army; the "waguers" had hold of their poles, and the "thrutchers"—two of us—were ready for work behind. A youngster straddled the apex of the cart, seated between two branches of oak, where he looked like a "Jack-in-the-Green." The signal was given to start, and we were off—no, not *we*—*they* were off; but one of the "thrutchers" was left behind. Not being able to see my way through the folds of ribbon that dangled and fluttered before my eyes, I got tripped by a stone that lay in my path, and pitched into a pool of water and slush that might have been placed there on purpose. I dare-say I should have laughed as loudly as I cried had anyone else been in the mess: but my holiday was over for that day. I crept home heart-broken—was stripped and put to bed, from which I could hear the jubilance of my late companions, which was galling to me. Worst of all, I had completely spoiled a sash ribbon that a young woman, a neighbour, used to tie round her waist when she took part in the pastoral duet of "Colin and Phebe" at the women's club. These events settled my rushcarting.

About this time Aaron Andrew's wife happened to "brew" for their own use. Aaron was a waggoner, who made long hours. Laborious employment, it was thought, required some kind of stimulant; and as Aaron had not the time to take his nightly "pint" at the publichouse, he imbibed his own "concoction" on his own hearth. There was no spirit drinking in those days, not in villages, except by habitual topers, who did nothing else. The beer which had been working in a mug until the surface was covered with a blister of barm, was deemed ready for "tunning," or, to use the modern term, "bottling." The daughter and I— she was only just my senior—it would appear, had made it up to have a fuddle. She got a tea cup, and diving under the barm, as we had seen her mother do, we commenced work. This is all I remember of the proceedings in the kitchen; but I have been told by more than one witness that we were both found on our backs as completely "stitched up" as if we had been at an election. As a matter of course we were put to bed to await a return of con-sciousness, and pay the penalty of our first spree. Our companions very soon got to know of our carousal; and we were freely taunted with the remark, "Eh, des bin dyunken'." I had noticed, even at that early age, that people who sometimes went on the fuddle for a week at a time, and went home each day to their meals, as though they had been working, paraded the road with a kind of swagger, as if getting drunk was something to be proud of. If their getting round was anything like mine was I could have made them welcome to their pride. It is now the fashion for those who care about their characters to conceal it as much as possible, leaving the " swaggering " to the lowest types of civilisation.

Now came the time of my introduction to Pole Lane classics. I was sent to school; John Goodier's modest academy for very young ladies, and very young gentlemen, being the place selected, because there was no other, for the exercise of the ruler and thimble in the development of my bumps. I was an adept pupil, and rose from the A. B. C.'s in such a short time that before I was five years old I took the first prize in spelling. The word was " victuals ; " the prize *three marbles*. Elated by this success, visions of academical honours, never to be attained, floated before my fancy ; and a prospect bright as a summer morn, opened before me. But a cloud drifted over the scene. The nation was without a crowned king ; and the coronation of William IV. was made an excuse for holidays everywhere. The day before this event took place was the last on which I attended John Goodier's school, or, indeed, any other day school. Great were the rejoicings, I remember, on the day of the coronation. The May Pole was taken down, and re-painted ; the vane and points re-gilded ; and all Failsworth turned out in its grandeur of holiday dress,—flags, banners, bands, and processions. The most conspicuous object in one of these pageants was a cart, on the sides of which a hand-loom had been erected. A weaver was seated at his work, and by his side a winder plying the bobbin-wheel. " God Save the King " was sung at each public-house door ; for the loyalty of that day must be kept damp. *Dryness* interfered with the weaver's work. It caused his yarn to snap ; and the winder alleged that it caused the weft so to snarl that he found it impossible to make good bobbins unless it was steeped in " fourpenny."

But pageantry and drink were not everything provided to celebrate the glorious event. An ox was roasted in front of the Crown and Cushion. The boiling parts were converted into " stew " to be served out to all comers, the almoner being a woman living near the scene of " dole." I was sent with a jug to get a quart of what the Yankees would call " beef juice." But the woman pushed me aside. " Nawe, thou mun ha' noane," she said ; " thy gron-feyther's a Jacobin." Heartbroken and empty, I returned home. I had been led to anticipate such a " blow out " as I had never had before ; and the disappointment was overwhelming. What had Jacobinism to do with an empty stomach ? I wondered ; or how was a child of five to reason out the cause that politics should operate as a kind of caste among poor people? From that day I began to *think*; but I have not yet arrived at the conclusion that we ought to be made responsible for the opinions held by our ancestors, or to suffer on account of their actions.

Taken away from school, I had to assist in the "bread-winning" by hawking from door to door. But that was mostly in winter. On summer days it would have been difficult to find me if I once got my heels to the back door, which afforded the readiest means of escape. Two of the younger branches of the Thorley family, the previously mentioned, were my companions; and the "Clough," with its facilities for swimming boats, was far more attractive than home. I remember the late Robert Thorley doing me a kindness that has often crossed my memory since, and we seldom met in after life without laughing over it.

It was Christmas time,—an old fashioned Christmas, when the waits did not hurry over their work on purpose to get through a lot of it; but stood around their neighbours' doors with the patience of donkeys, and sang the "Christmas Hymn" with becoming slowness, and with a reverent spirit. The snow lay thick upon the ground on the morning that I had to turn out with my little basket of oranges, which I was to dispose of at the price of "two for threehaupence." The air was crisp and keen; and as a protection from the cold I had a check napkin tied round my head; another was pinned round my shoulders for a shawl; and shod with a pair of clogs that were miniature stilts, I had to face the winter morn to go my round. I had called at Thorley's, who lived only across the bridge from the "Rocks;" had said my "two for threehaupence," —nothing more; made a sale; then set out for "Pee Fletcher's," the next house. But the snow had so accumulated on the bottoms of my clogs that I found locomotion to be impossible. Down I dropped at the corner of Walmsley's garden wall; and my limbs being benumbed by cold I could not regain my feet. In my strait the only thing I could do was to yell; and I daresay I exerted my lungs in a creditable manner. Robert Thorley was coming out of the house at the time; and hearing my well-developed treble, picked me up out of the snow, swung me on his back, basket and all, and carried me home. I think that was the last time I followed the occupation of a pedlar. In the kindness of her heart my mother bought me a screw money-box with the penny out of the threehalfpence I had drawn; and putting the halfpenny inside, made a Christmas gift to me of what I was to regard as the foundation of a fortune. But a stick of liquorice was too tempting for the foundation to be laid just then.

The next event in my life of any importance, was our removal from Failsworth to Hollinwood, a distance of something like three-quarters of a mile. This to me was a delightful change. We had got out of the hole, and were now on a level with other people. The house we were to inhabit had not been vacated when our cart arrived. It was Saturday night, and the wife was baking. One of the sons was weaving,—a lame youth who walked with a crutch. A companion, also lame, and who walked with a crutch, was sitting on the loom-rail; and I began to wonder if I had been cast among a community of cripples; and would I have to go upon crutches as well. How the double flitting went on during the night I never knew, as I was sent off to a shake-down bed; but on the Sunday morning I found that we had the domicile to ourselves. I made an early exploration of the neighbourhood, and discovered that our house was one of a row of such, standing close to the towing path of the Peak Forest canal. There was a farmhouse on the opposite side of the canal; a spacious orchard, the trees in which were covered with bloom, ran to the edge of the water; a thorn fence, well-grown, and in which I looked for birds nests, was within a few yards of the door; beyond this was a carpet of green meadow, and a cornmill; and when a new "chum" gave me a bite of his butter-cake, I began to realise, or thought I did, what Paradise was before the Fall.

I was assisted in my explorations of the neighbourhood about my new home by the young gentleman who had ingratiated him-self so agreeably into my favour. He had an intimate acquaintance with every spot that was sacred to childhood; showed me the hedge in which the wild convolvulus grew; the rivulet by the mill that had always been a mystery because it lost itself after entering a sough near the gate that led into old Smethurst's farm-yard; pointed out a crab tree that in the season yielded abundance of fruit which was never allowed to ripen, and gave little boys "what for" if they ate too much of it. He had himself suffered from over indulgence in this sour edible; but always forgot it when the season came round. I was shown the mill pond which was stored with gold fish that on hot days were to be seen floating on the surface; and we might catch them in the early morning before the miller's family were astir. For assisting in "housing" the hay, when we were big enough, we could share the privilege of entering the farmer's orchard, and picking up apples that had been blown from the trees. But I should see the cherries when they were ripe, and in clusters on the one tree. If I would be a good lad, and go for milk, and never tease the dog, nor "shoo" the hens, "Owd Betty" would not forget to give me a bunch; and if she knew I was hungry, she would accompany the gift with a delicious oatcake "thumb-buttercake," with such heaps of butter spread over it as to show the marks of my teeth. I was in a land of luxury!

My companion promised to initiate me into the usages of their boy society, which might be of a character different to what I had been accustomed to in the *country* I had left. Had I played "chub-i'th'-hole" with marbles? No. Had I played "pipes?" No. Had I tossed with buttons? No. Didn't I know the difference betwixt a "one-ter," and a "two-ter?" No. "Poor little fellow!" his looks seemed to say, "he knows nowt!" If I was not going to school after breakfast time he would show me favourite gaps in the hedges round about; the corner of old Fletcher's garden, where the poultry congregated most, and dropped their prettiest feathers; the "pig-cote," unused for its proper purpose, in which older boys met on winter nights, and told "boggart-tales" until they were so frightened that their parents had to fetch them home at bedtime. I had not long been a resident in the locality before I was permitted to pass the portals of that mysterious mansion.

We parted; my companion to go to his porridge, but not before he had thoroughly interviewed me on matters affecting the prestige of the juvenile society of that place and period. His questions were put in a manner meant to be serious; and my answers were expected to be given honestly and straight-forward.

"Cont' feight?" was the first query put.

I had to confess that I had not had the least experience in any kind of pugilistic entertainment.

"If thou conno feight," was the warning given, "be thick wi' Jack Thuston. He throwed Jammie Bradley o'er his yead yesterday; an' he lit i'th' sink. Cont' run?"

With a little natural pride I told him that I had often led the race with my *cutter-leg* (hoop), and hoped to improve in running as I grew stronger.

"'Cose we wanten someb'dy fort' *bret* (beat) Charlie Hyde," he went on. "He's th' don. Yo'n ha' t' run round Jimmie fielt; an' if Will Standrin catches thee he'll chuck thee into th' pit. But there isno' mich wayter in it. If owd Billy Andrey, th' lock-tenter, catches thee throwin' stones i'th' *cut* (canal) he'll squeeze thee till thou feels empty. An' if Jim of Ash'n (the constable) catches thee pooin any stones off th' wall, he'll tak thee to their house, an' gie thee a good hoidin, an' a bit o' sweetstuff."

Grateful for the instruction and advice I had received, as well as for the offers of boyish friendship, which is sometimes more genuine than that of maturer years, I turned to the parapet of the canal bridge, against which I leaned, whilst I indulged in a little meditation. I knew it would be of no use going home just then, although the clink of the porridge pan would have been a welcome sound, so I looked abroad on the landscape that spread itself out before me; and listened to the drowsy sounds of village life on a Sabbath morn. There was the tinkle of the escape water from the canal locks, varied in its tone as the summer breeze swept around it; the squeak of the Tinker Lane pump, as some housewife plied the handle for the breakfast water; the lowing of the cows on old Smethurst's farm; and anon the ding ding of the church bell, a sound I had never listened to before, because Failsworth did not possess a church at that time. These novelties to the auricular sense had their charm; and as I gazed upon the empty boats that dozed on the basin, now and then wakening each other from sleep by a slight bump, the poetry of a childish soul stirred within me. But on turning round I saw my mother's cap, and blessing the face that was inside of it—a dusky rose in folds of white cambric—I flew to her side. It was the signal for porridge time.

I found my brother already on his chair at the table, and waving aloft his spoon, awaiting orders to charge. As we were strangers to the place, a little girl fetched the milk, and confided to me the sad intelligence that her sister, who had died of fever, was to be buried that day. Poor Eliza! that was the little errand girl's name; it was not long after when a mother's screams startled the "fowt;" her child was in flames—she was burnt to death. I believe I loved that girl with a childish love, because I sorrowed for her as if she had been my sister.

I was deprived of the opportunity of further exploring the neighbourhood that day, as I had to be bundled off to the Sunday school—a new experience to me—in charge of a bigger boy, who was exceedingly patronising. He bounced about his spelling; and could "bret" any lad i' readin th' "begats." My mother had polished my clogs for the occasion, and stitched a frill to my jacket collar, that made me look like a daisy. What a school house it was that seemed to open its dusky arms to receive me! The building had at one time been a hatter's workshop. Now a portion of it was a stable; and we could hear the kicking of the horses when "silence" was called, or when we were at prayers. The boys were located on the basement, and the girls occupied the upper storey, so much of the flooring having been cut away in the centre as to accommodate a pulpit, so small, and so ludicrous in its situation, that when the " holder forth " for the day popped up his head, we likened him to a "jack-in-the-box." We could see the girls behind the balustrade at singing time. Bless the memory of their pretty faces, and their white pinafores, that I could compare to nothing less refreshing than a cool breeze in summer.

"Mind thoose breek, Benny, or else thou'll tumble o'er 'em;" was the caution administered to me on entering the passage leading into the school. " They're what we makken sparrow traps on ith' winter, we'n had 'em out o' owd Bill Hadcroft's stable. Thou munno' shout 'Lovely Jane' when thou sees owd Bill's wife. If thou does hoo'll skelp thee."

" What art' coed ? " demanded a little bow-legged teacher as I was ushered into that worthy's presence.

" Benny," I replied.

" Benny what ? "

" Brearley."

" What cont' read in ? "

" Th' Testyment."

" Thou'rt a little chap for t' be ith' Testyment. We'n try what thou con do." With that he opened a book—"hapchance," as my father would have said—and pointing to a page, he said," " Read thoose four vesses."

I read them,—ran away with the words. The test was as easy to me as it would be now; and the result was that I had to be enrolled in the Bible class—the highest in the school.

" Hast any marbles i' thy pocket ? " enquired the teacher to whom I had been transferred.

" Nawe," I replied.

" Buttons ? "

" Nawe."

" Pipes ? " *

" Nawe."

" Wipe thy nose, an' goo at back o'th' desk. I think thou'll do." This was my formal introduction to the class, where I received two pinches in the rear before I got to my seat.

* The teacher meant bits of pipe stems for playing with, as with marbles, unknown now-a-days.

Having settled myself in my corner, where I had to dodge what I took for a wasp, but which proved to be nothing more harmful than a stable fly, I sat in nervous anticipation of the first lesson. I was asked by the next boy if I could spell " gimlet," and on my giving the letters correctly, I received the assurance that if I could spell every word like that, and being a new boy, I would have to " feight." The others were not going to be put out in that manner. I was further questioned. Did I " count round " when the class was engaged in the reading lesson ? I replied to the effect that I did not, as I was ignorant of what the term meant. The boy explained—

" After thou's read a vess, an' thou wants t' know which is th' next thou should read, so ut thou con labbor it, thou *counts round* th' class for t' see. If th' taicher catches thee, an' he never looks at his book when it comes to hard words, he'll gi'e thee sich a rap."

" But why doesno' he look at his book when it comes to hard words ? " I wished to know.

The reply was significant.

" Becose he conno' tell us what they are, an' he lets us say 'em as we liken."

Scriptual names of one or two syllables our teacher could easily dispose of, and he discharged the duty with much dignity. *Moab* he pronounced as if spelt *Mobe*; *Noah* as if spelt *Noe*, and I remember, when a boy pronounced *Gamaliel* as if spelt *Gammylile*, his superior's attention was fixed on other objects than his book. Perhaps he was looking out for boys who were " counting round."

In the first reading lesson I acquitted myself so well that the teacher patted my head ; and I received an intimation from the next boy that I would be wanted in the " Bradley," that was a large field opposite the school, at " locin' time." I guessed what I was wanted for ; but took no further notice of it ; I was not going to have my pinafore and frill mauled on a Sunday. I was a little nervous, too, when the time drew near, and felt afraid that I might be " two'd " for being a coward. I came by no harm as things turned out.

After the reading lesson we had something like half an hour's rest, which leisure was devoted, as I could hear, to plotting mischief, and talking about it. My next boy offered to get me off the " meeting " in the Bradley for a bit of liquorice. Fortunately I had about six inches in my pocket—very dry it was ; and we managed to split it in two. That proved to be a peace offering. The boy kept his word. I have thought since it was only a case of levying "black-mail," and that I need not have been in fear of molestation. We turned upon matters more congenial to my disposition.

" How dun they feed *buzzarts* (butterflies) at Pow? " the boy enquired. Failsworth seldom got its proper name. It was mostly called " Pow," from its May *pole*.

I had never kept, nor even caught " buzzarts," so could not give him the information he required.

" We feeden 'em o' sugar an' meal here," I was told. " An' thou con buy a box for a penny at Jack Lawton's, like a little house wi' a dur to."

I had been in Hollinwood only a piece of a day; and yet I began to think I was getting to know as much of its juvenile society as I knew of that appertaining to my native village. I was being educated rapidly; but soon discovered that there were branches of this kind of education that I had not access to without paying smartly for it. As yet I knew nothing of " trillil; " " hommer an' block; " " Little Johnny Lingo; " "playin at hosses; " and "towns." My ignorance of these institutions was sport for the class; and I was tauntingly asked if I had done sucking, or had I played with dolls. Did I ever catch " canary buzzarts ? " Were there any of these moths at " th' Pow ? " Did I ever turn in a rope-walk? Did I ever " poo at th' idle-bant ? " None of these things had I ever done; and I began to feel that my early experiences had been exceedingly limited.

Spelling time came, and it was the " hard word day." I found it was not called that for nothing. The words given to us *were* hard, very hard. No doubt they would have been sufficiently difficult to spell if they had been correctly pronounced by the teacher. But when the word " erysipelas " was pronounced " erysipallus," with the *y* sounded as in *try*, and accentuated on " pal," it was like being put on a false scent; and serves to show how little the spelling we did would be of any good to us in after life. Neither jealousy nor heartburning resulted from that spelling lesson, as not a word was spelt correctly. Even " eschew," which was pronounced " eskew," and was said to mean " skew-wift," challenged the orthographical abilities of the best " scholar " in the class.

School hours over I was shown the nearest way home. This was gratifying to me, as hunger had prompted me to speculate upon what there would be for dinner. My expectations had been considerably raised by my early morning's experiences. Was not

Hollinwood a richer country than Failsworth? Why, there were two butcher's shops in the former for one in the latter; so there must be better doings where I was. When I reached home, and had opened the door, what a grateful odour assailed my olfactory sense. I would scarcely believe it was real. But when my brother assured me that he had seen it " boil o'er; " and that there was a canal round the rim of the crust, I knew I was in the presence of a potato pie. And what a large oven it was baking in! None of your two-muffin-wides, but a *three*. Hurray!

"Dunno mak sich a noise, Benny," said my mother, in a suppressed voice; "thou'll wakken that deead wench next dur."

"Lemme look i'th' oon, an' then I winno'," I bargained.

The favour was granted me, and I had a peep into the oven. The pie did not look the size it was from the oven being such a large one; but it might be big enough. There was the canal round the rim that my brother had spoken of; and the crust was browning beautifully. A suspicion fell upon my mind that was most discomforting.

"Mother," I said, "is Martin comin'?" This person was a well-known twister-in for weavers; and an extra quality of dinner had to be provided on the occasion of his visits. He could "stand his corner," too, at anything; but a potato pie was his favourite dish.

My mother smiled.

"Thou doesno' think Martin goes a twinin-in ov a Sunday, doesta, Benny?" she said. "Besides, we ha'no wun-on yet."

This was a relief to me; and I went to "shoo" some ducks on the canal to get the time over.

I have been at banquets when the highest in the land have been present. I know the flavour of turtle. I have had salmon and green peas when such dainties have scarcely been come-at-able. I have tasted game when it has been "gamy," and washed down with champagne. But give me the appetite of those early days, and place a potato pie before me, with buttermilk to pour on the concrete; and instead of its taking two hours to gorge myself, I would engage to leave my plate so clean that the hungriest dog would pass it by without a wag of its tail, in less time than it takes an alderman to gobble his "green fat," or my Lady Mumbles to get through her bit of chicken.

When I heard the clank of the oven door, I hoisted the white flag to the ducks, and flew to the place where the fight of peace was throngest. The next minute I was scalding my mouth into blisters. But what was a mouth fit for if it would not stand scalding? Hopes were raised in me that day which were too grand to be realised, as the augury of better things was of the brightest. I did not go to school in the afternoon, as my mother had discovered a loose "shingle" on my trousers; so I had to be sent upstairs while it was being "fixed," a circumstance that I did not much regret, as I could watch the funeral from the chamber window.

My Sunday School experiences grew to be of the most delightful character. A few weeks wore off the strangeness of the situation. I was no longer regarded by my schoolmates as an alien, but received into their confidence with open arms. Not only had I not to "feight," but was taken under the protection of the champion of the class, with whom I shared liquorice and barley sugar when he was in funds. This youth was dull at learning, but had acquired the newest method of giving the "leg" to an antagonist when contending in the "Bradley." I had frequently to go over a chapter with him previous to the lesson, that he might get at my way of pronouncing hard names, which he as often forgot, and blundered over them in a most ludicrous manner. To add to his confusion, and I may say ours, as well, we had a change of teachers, the newly installed being a Welshman. He was a good hearted young fellow, almost fresh from the Principality; and the mess he made with the English language as we spoke it at the time, would, but for his kindness, have got us many a sound thrashing. But I do not remember his ever using the stick. He was a "journey-man" shoemaker by trade, and worked for the principal employer in the locality. I had been to his "shop" one day for a "haupo'th o' wax," when I saw him at his work. He bargained with me at once that I should take his place at school when reading lessons, and he would stand by me. As remuneration for my labour he would give me sixpence in Whit-week, for "Whissunday brass." This was too good an offer to be declined; and for several successive Sundays I had to stand upon a form as "monitor" to the Bible class.

Whit-week came, and as one day succeeded another I might have been seen in a field overlooking a certain garden belonging to a shoemaker, in hopes of receiving the promised sixpence. Friday morning came, and still my visions of wealth had not been realised. We had to walk round the village that day, the muster called for nine o'clock. I was on my look out in the meadow earlier than usual, and it was so near porridge time that my anxiety had reached a feverish pitch. When I felt that it would not be safe to remain on the watch any longer, for fear of missing my homely breakfast, I saw a pair of shirt-sleeves, and a face that could not be mistaken. The next minute the sixpence was flung over the hedge; and I ran home, the richest and happiest boy in Hollinwood.

I could not keep the secret of my good fortune. I confided it to my companions when we met at school, some of whom vowed eternal friendship. But one envious youth called attention to my pardonable vanity by remarking to the other boys,—"See, waggerin'." It was our way of applying the term "swaggering."

We set out for our "walking round" with the freshness of birds on their morning wing; and the clatter we made on the pavement cannot be heard now-a-days. With few exceptions the school was "clogged," some of the soles being so set with "stumps," that it was a feat to be the best at "striking fire." These flint-and-steel exercises interfered with the order and sedateness of the procession, and occasionally brought down the stick.

We had a wearying "trapes" that day; and I began to feel that the feast of currant bread which we were to have at the finish was getting farther off. We had so much calling and singing to do on the way, camping wherever there was a bit of green, or in front of a house of more than ordinary pretentions, that the "sickness of the heart," arising from the "hope deferred," became intolerable. But when at last we turned the Post-office corner, and knew there could not be another calling place, our tired limbs felt refreshed, and our clogs grew lighter. A few minutes longer and it would be "Oh, be joyful" with us. The first glance at the stack of slices of currant bread, or I might describe them as thick slabs, was as a first sight of land to a wearied voyager. But what when our ivory snaps had closed on the first mouthful; and the "tot" of wine that had never known a vineyard, was simmering at our parched lips?

Ye children of the present day who have your milk and buns, and a field to play in, and have not to carry small loads of timber over hard highways for three or four hours without a bite, after an indifferent breakfast; who go by rail to scenes strange and romantic; or caged in covered lurries where you can sing like birds, for a nearer "outing," and have your refreshments spread upon the grass, try to realise for yourselves the hardship, that was supposed to be pleasure, which we had to endure in the "good old times" when William the Fourth was king. A return to those days would sharpen your appetites when you turn up your noses at a crust, and fling it in the street.

I became so attached to school that I never could be prevailed upon to play the truant, not even if there was the attraction of a "boat-swim" in the Bower brook. Had I been led away I might have got into the hands of the churchwardens, who were always on the alert for Sabbath-breakers. Two of my companions were caught on one occasion, and had to do "penance," such as it was, in a part of the church where they could best be seen. I remember one Sunday I was unshod. My mother had taken my clogs to the clogging on the Saturday, and the men were over-crowded with work. My clogs were not touched. My parent, seeing me grieve that I could not attend school, borrowed a pair of clogs from a girl who wore shoes on Sundays, but they caused me to be the butt of the class, as it was considered to be effeminate, and beneath boyish dignity, to wear "wenches' clogs."

Hollinwood had its "Band." Do not laugh, dear reader, for to have a band in those days was a very important matter. You would have thought so if you had heard and seen it leading up St. Margaret's scholars on a "charity day," to the tune of "Owd Billy," occasionally changed to "Halifax," then a favourite hymn tune. Often did I wish this band would lead us up, that we might have the opportunity of seeing their brass instruments flashing in the sun, "ever so far" in front of us, and of making very random speculations upon the length of the procession. But we were only poor "ranters" and could not afford to pay.

The uniform adopted by these musical gentlemen was a blue swallow-tail coat with brass buttons, white trousers, and a black beaver with a yellow band. They were in our eyes princes who had condescended to come amongst poor people. Poor Jammie Booth, he played the long trumpet, and his legs were too short to keep in step, and as the rest of the players stepped to the music, Jammie found himself at the finish about half the tune behind. He ultimately gave it up. His diminutive stature, he would observe, "would no' afford splitting up any furr." Some of these "band chaps" are still living, and one in particular occupies the eminent position of bandmaster to a volunteer corps.

But we juveniles must have a band of our own, that we might make engagements to lead up scholars or Odd-fellows, and lay up the money we earned by our playing to buy instruments with. But we had forgotten that we should want the instruments first. However, we must be content with make-shifts for a start. Accordingly I furnished myself with a whistle, a common one; another had what he called a French whistle, rather of a fancy make, but with

B

no better music in it than mine had, because neither could play a tune of itself, and we could not assist them one jot.

Our band would have been incomplete without bass instruments, or one at least; and this desideratum was supplied by a cow's horn which had done duty behind a huckster's donkey. The rest of the instruments, with one exception, were whistles of various keys. The exception was a flute which the smallest boy in the "troupe" had learnt to play. How I envied that boy, and his playing of "Owd Billy," and "In a cottage near a wood," which I tried ineffectually to blow out of my whistle! After a few weeks' practice, to the annoyance of a would-be quiet neighbourhood, we made our first engagement. It was "pancake day," and we had been invited by my mother to play at our house, each of us to have a pancake, and a "tot" of "Old Bardsley's hush," as an honorarium for our services. In the early forenoon we mustered in the "fowt" of the "Old Sheaf" in Wicken-tree Lane, and played up to our door, followed by the yelling of children, and the barking of dogs all the way. On reaching our house we formed in a ring opposite the door after the custom of other bands, and struck up nobody knew what beside ourselves. I could see my father in the loomhouse with his hands to his ears, which I thought was rather ominous. The medley finished we entered the house, and dispatched our pancakes as rapidly as they were made,—partook of our "barley-tea," and formed under the clock for a *finale*. The blowing was something immense. The performer on the cow's horn had got entangled amongst the clock weights, and had stopped the clock. At this moment my father emerged from the loom-house, with a stick concealed behind him. He always carried it that way when he meant special business. "Heaw soon will th' tune be finished?" he demanded sternly, "becose I mean startin some music of another sort. Old damnel yo, you'n stop th' clock wi' yor noise. If yo' are no' off eaut o' this heause in a quarter of a minit I'll help yo' eaut." We needed no further advice. In a moment we were scattered in the "fowt" like a flock of hens when a dog has given them warning. I believe that was the only engagement we were ever asked to fulfil. Our band got dis-banded soon after, and was never re-formed. Music had lost its charm.

And now came the time that I had to be put to work. I had *played* at pulling the "idle bant" when the clogger's apprentices were cross-cutting timber for soles; I had *played* at turning a handle in the Bower Lane rope-walk until my hands were blistered all over; but now I must *work*, as I was getting too big to run in the fields, or raise dust in the lanes. I was put to the bobbin-wheel. How I hated being chained to the stool! and how I suffered from the effects of having "bad bobbins" flung at my head! I have before me as I sit at the table the scissors I used at that time, now upwards of fifty years ago. I have used them since—as a weaver; as a warper; as sub-editor of a newspaper; and during the last fifteen years as editor of the journal that bears my name.

The old bobbin-wheel was never in the right place. I moved it all over the house; and one fine summer day, when I could hear other children at skipping-rope, and marbles, I took it into the "fowt," and trundled the detestable thing about in imitation of a scissors-grinder's machine. But my fun was not long to be enjoyed. As I was in the act of calling out "sithors to grind," I felt a grab at my hair, followed by a lift behind that knocked me over my "show." The experiment was never repeated. At another time my father was out of bobbins; and I was on the hunt for something good. My mother, I knew, had made a gooseberry pie, and it had been cut into. I had discovered, after much searching, that the dainty was on the top shelf behind the kitchen door. I made a ladder of the cross-bars of the door, and mounted. Just as I got a mouthful of pie the looms stopped. "Bobbins," my father shouted. No response. "Bobbins," was repeated. I durst not stir. Then I heard the seat-board bang against the wall, and felt myself "in for it." "That little d——l's off out again," he said, as he saw the vacant stool. But turning round he beheld my hands grasping the top of the kitchen door. My descent was but the work of a second, being accelerated by a hand that knew how to inflict a blow. Giving me up as a bad job, so far as bobbin-winding was concerned, I was sent to the factory, where I was to learn spinning. I became a "piecer." But the atmosphere of the mill did not suit my delicate constitution. I had to leave soon after I had been promoted to a "middle piecer." But I think the style of living I had to put up with had as much to do with breaking down my health as anything beside.

Factory operatives of the present day have no idea of the hardships endured by those of their class from forty to fifty years ago. At that time there was scarcely any limit to the hours of labour. It was common enough to start the engine at half-past five, and not leave off until seven. The mills of that period were low, and badly ventilated. In some of them gas had not been introduced. In the one I worked at, candles were used, and were so scantily distributed as only to "make darkness visible." The piecer's watchfulness, aided by a tolerable length of strap, had to make up for the absence of light. Winter was a dreadful time in those days. "Lucifer" matches had not then been invented, or had not found their way into the homes of the poor, and the flint-and-steel was a luxury confined to the better-doing. If the house-fire had gone out at night we had no means of lighting it in the morning except by enclosing a candle in a home-made paper lantern, and going about the neighbourhood in search of an accessible fire. If none could be found at that early hour we had to encounter the severest weather, sometimes fasting, and often without having had anything warm. There were no coffee stalls at street corners; no brilliantly lighted public house "vaults," where the adult could creep in, and warm his nose over rum and coffee; no street lamps to cheer the dreary way—our constant company being cold, darkness, and semi-starvation. Often have I been invited to shelter under a girl's cloak, and take a bite of her butter-cake, when either could ill be spared. But the poor were good almoners to the more needy; and the world knew not the extent of their bounty.

Whilst working at this mill a lamentable incident occurred that made a deep impression on my mind at the time, and has had a determining influence on my after life. We had a temporary breakdown one winter's day, which caused something like an hour's cessation from work. The Hollinwood reservoir, a broad expanse of water that supplies the canal, was partially frozen over, and a portion of it was strong enough for sliding upon. The temptation to venture upon the ice was too strong to be resisted, and nearly the whole of the factory hands were enjoying themselves in an atmosphere not heated by steam. I was passionately fond of the ice, but cautious nevertheless, and never could be induced to trust myself where a fall would make a "clock-face," or where there was any undulation when a skater passed over. Could I have mustered a pair of skates it might have been different; but I had to content myself with a weaver's spindle let into the clog sole of my left foot, with spikes driven into the sole of my right foot clog, by which to propel me along. Thus equipped I have missed many a meal-hour in my eargerness for the pastime, "doing" my eccentric spin on the canal from Bradley Bent bridge to the "Crime" water, a distance of over two miles. But on this occasion I had to be satisfied with a slide; and right merrily we went at it, as only youngsters know how, performing "little-daddy," which in some parts of England goes by the name of "knocking at the cobbler's door," and other popular feats.

We had not been long on the reservoir before we heard a cry—"There's somebody in." Yes, there was. In the distance, and where the ice could hardly have been strong enough to have held a cat, poor Dick Hargreaves, a little piecer employed in the same room as myself, was struggling for life. We knew what the end must be. There was not the slightest chance of rescue, as there were no boats on the reservoir as there are now, nor any other means of saving from drowning. On the Chapel-road stood his father, watching his drowning boy fight for existence, powerless himself to respond to the call for help it was impossible to render. Young as I was I could imagine the father's feelings as tearless he stood, but with an intensely wild stare, waiting for the last struggle. It came; the water was motionless, and we knew by that sign that all was over. The father heaved a deep sigh, and walked from the spot as if he knew not whither he was going.

In the evening an unusual procession was seen moving up Tinker Lane. It consisted of a number of men bearing on their shoulders a boat which they had brought from the Bower Mill. These were led up by the drowned boy's father, carrying a lantern. They were going to search for the body, which was found near the place where the unfortunate youth went down. The scene was a weird one to me, and resembled, as I had pictured in my mind, a life-boat rescue at sea. Since that time, though now nearly fifty years ago, I have avoided venturing on ice as a mad dog shuns water.

Before leaving the cotton mill I had the good fortune to make my first acquaintance with the earlier works of Charles Dickens. Our manager, who was a reading man, was subscribing to period-ically issued numbers of the "Pickwick Papers." He had seen me in the breakfast half-hour poring over the contents of a dirty rag of paper,—not that the matter was dirty,—but the paper itself was oiled, and worn from its being constantly carried about in my pocket. This was "Cleave's Gazette," published weekly at a penny, a sum I managed to screw out of my threepence a fortnight "odd brass." This reading the manager had noticed; and he generously offered me an early perusal of the "Pickwick Papers," on the condition that I fetched the numbers as they were due from a little stationer's shop near the Navigation Inn. This was a double pleasure to me, as in addition to reading the pamphlet I could have half-an-hour's breathing outside the mill. Dickens assisted in lightening the burden of a weary time. I gathered fresh

life from his admirable writings; and even then began to look into
the distant future with the hope that at sometime I might be
enabled to track his footsteps, however far I might be behind.
This prospect constantly buoyed up my hopes; and when at last I
was taken away from the mill I felt a regret that by this proceeding
I had sacrificed a glorious opportunity of making myself known in
the world. But my health had to be the first thing to be considered, because I was reduced to the condition of a lantern, and
even imagined I could see through my hands. I often caught my
mother in tears as she sat gazing at my wasted form.

Being long in the legs for my age, I was put to the hand-loom at
home, and on a class of work that could not well be spoiled. It
was a mixture of cotton and worsted, and known by the name of
" Shrouds." I suppose by that it was intended for the meagre
clothing of the dead. The manufacturer was a nice old gentleman
named Aaron Mills, and had his " putting out " place in Ashton.
Many years after that time the memory of " Old Aaron " had to
pose for the character of " Aaron Hartley " in my story, " The
Layrock of Langley Side." A very amusing incident occurred at
the time I was weaving these " shrouds." A little fellow, a
neighbour, who wove the same kind of goods, had been to Ashton
with his work, and was returning by the canal side, with his wallet
well stuffed with worsted, when his eye caught sight of something
in front that quite fascinated him. It was a young woman well
known in the neighbourhood of " Waterhouses," and who was
remarkable for her fine personal appearance, stepping over a muddy
place, she displayed such a splendid development of white-
stockinged ankle that the little weaver became suddenly intoxi-
cated with the sight, and reeled into the canal, where he might
have been drowned had it not been for the assistance of two boat-
men who happened to be near. They got him out of the water,
and took him home in their boat. I saw the enamoured little
fellow seated on a cross plank as the boat passed our loomhouse
window, and he presented a deplorable spectacle. It was said that
the young woman alluded to assisted in the rescue, as she heard
him say that he would tumble into the canal again for another such
a sight.

I was now earning seven-and-sixpence a week, and things were
looking up on " Cut side." But this gleam of prosperity soon
became obscured. Work in " shrouds " fell off, and silk was no
better, if not worse. Weavers had often to wait weeks for warps,
and changes were frequent. " Our folks " were put to great shifts

to keep the cart going. Having no other work to do I employed myself in dragging a wagon laden with coals from the Limeside coal pits, a distance of nearly a mile; having to go twice for a "tub," for which I received threepence remuneration. On one occasion the threepence thus earned had to provide a dinner for the four of us,—twopennyworth of bacon, and one pennyworth of potatoes. A little of such experience might do some of our youngsters good. Boys of that period did not smoke cigars, nor wear broadcloth, nor had they pluck to behave rudely to older people. Stern lessons were being taught that have not since been forgotten.

But a brighter day succeeded this night of poverty. I was growing into a "felly lad," and work was better. I had been attending a night school kept by a cousin of mine in Wrigley Head. Here I learned to write; and my Sunday School companions looked on with wonder at my progress in penmanship, as they were only taught on the Sabbath. The night school was held in a four-loomed loomhouse, with one loom in a corner, on which our schoolmaster wove, taught us our lessons in arithmetic, and "set copies." My uncle played the flute, and often interfered with our studies by his merry "tootling. This cousin succeeded in obtaining the mastership of the Failsworth Old School, the scene of my early struggles with the alphabet. He held the situation during his life.

In 1842, four years after I had left the factory, the "great strike" took place, an event which some of our neighbours had been expecting a long time before, and were, in their way, prepared to meet. During the four years chartism had been rife, and the strike was its culmination. The *Northern Star*, the only newspaper that appeared to circulate anywhere, found its way weekly to the Cut side, being subscribed for by my father and five others. Every Sunday morning these subscribers met at our house to hear what prospect there was of the expected "smash-up" taking place. It was my task to read aloud so that all could hear at the same time; and the comments that were made on the events apparently foreshadowed would have been exceedingly edifying to me were I to hear them now. A Republic was to take the place of the "base, bloody, and brutal Whigs," and the usurpers of all civil rights, the Lords. The Queen was to be dethroned, and the president of a Republic take her place. This would be a very easy task. Ten thousand trained pikemen would sweep England through; and Hollinwood could furnish a contingent of at least a thousand. My father did not encourage these "physical forceist" ideas. Having been at Waterloo, he knew what fighting meant, especially on battlefields where they could not run away. But perhaps it was his fun to be a non-acquiescing listener. Besides reading the *Northern Star* on Sunday mornings, my Saturday afternoons were occupied by more arduous work. I had to turn my father's grindstone whilst rebelliously-disposed amateur soldiers ground their pikes. Had he refused the use of the grindstone he might have been suspected of being a traitor to the cause. I remember well the faces of the men who brought pikes to be ground, and their neglect to give me any remuneration for my labour. But what did that matter, they were patriots, and things would come round in grand style some day.

There was a man from the neighbourhood of Ashton-under-Lyne of the name of Fenton who furnished our people with these pikes, often carrying a wooden model with him; and a man named Kay, to whom we applied the prefix of "Doctor," because he sold pills in the Oldham market place. These two combined kept the sedition pot boiling until the time that active measures were taken to place Feargus O'Connor in Whitehall. But the storm burst upon the country ere it was expected, and we found the English Statute Book confronted by mob law. All kinds of work ceased as if from a stroke of paralysis, and in a day or two a smoking chimney was not to be seen.

I was at that time weaving velvet, and could have earned, if I had had my own way, very fair wages, considering the period. But I was kept back for obvious reasons. If I had earned more than a certain sum, employers would have taken advantage of it, and a reduction would probably have taken place. So I eked out my time with fishing opposite our own door. But prices of weaving had fallen notwithstanding—fallen considerably, which induced me to join the strikers. I entered into the movement with all the zest of youth, and rushed into danger heedless of consequences. I was present at "plug-drawings" everywhere, disguised by appearing in my shirt sleeves, my paper cap, and the leather apron I wore at my velvet loom. I managed by these means to keep out of the hands of the constables. We had a month of Sundays; and when at last the strike came to an end, and people began to dribble to their work, it was not without some reluctance that I dusted my loom, and resumed, what a neighbour gave the name to, my "three-and-one-bump." But the strike had proved beneficial in one respect. If it had not made the "People's Charter" the law of the land, it had enhanced the price of velvet weaving at least twenty per cent.

We had scarcely got settled down to work when a report came that a successful attempt had been made to renew the strike in Ashton and Stalybridge, for—

> " Doctor Kay
>   Had come that way,
> From Ashton, Hyde, and Denton,
>   Who swore that troops
>   Of Feargus' dupes
> Were being led up by Fenton ;
>   And that they meant,
>   Where'er they went,
> The strike flame to rekindle,
>   Till from Oldham Edge
>   To Stalybridge
> They'd stopped both loom and spindle."

My father, and his neighbour, Phil o' Berry, set out to Ashton at once, to see for themselves if the news were true. They found the mills at work, and nobody apparently idling. On passing a stationer's shop Phil's attention was arrested by a portrait of Joseph Raynor Stephens in the window. By accident or design Stephens was standing on his head.

"It's no use gooin' any fur'r, Brayly," said Phil ; "they'n turned Stephens th' wrong side up. It's domino wi' th' strike."

As a set-off to this flow of prosperity my mother was seized with a violent fever, and was held in bed by it for nearly a month. What an anxious time this was to me, for I did not believe that, had she died, there was another woman on earth could have taken her place either as a mother or a wife. She was everything to me ; and not all the romance that ever heated the blood of youth could have supplanted her in my affections. When it was made known to me that the malady had reached a critical stage, I was overwhelmed with visions of what our home would be without her. I had known other boys who had been left motherless go to rags both in clothing and morals, and feared that such would be my fate. It was on a Saturday afternoon in summer when the news was whispered to me by a neigbour woman who had not left the sick bed since early morning. She added that I had better not continue weaving, as the noise of the loom might " put her off."

I knew what that meant, and felt the full force of that ominous teaching. I covered up my cloth, and went to unburden my heart in the solitude of a green bank by the canal side, to which we had given the name of " Th' Little Garden," and where I had gathered wild raspberries in happier days. On this spot I lay in dreamy and tearful melancholy till dusk, dreading to go home; and the question was ever uppermost, "What shall we do without my mother?" I had been educated at her knee. I had been taught loving-kindness by her looks; and learnt to hope for a bright future by her whisperings of heaven. Now all would be a blank to me. I was disturbed in my gloomy reverie by the vision of a neighbour girl approaching me. I guessed by her looks she was not the bearer of bad news, and I was not wrong. "Benny," she said, before I had time to ask her anything, "thy mother's better." " God bless thee, D—— !" was all that I could utter; and it need not be wondered at if the joy of that moment kindled in my breast the first scintillation of a boyish love.

My parent's health continued to progress after the turn it had taken; and the following Saturday I had the pleasure of seeing the familiar face beaming from its wonted corner by the fireside; the russet red of her cheeks toned down by her illness to a delicate rose, approaching the sweet blonde of a younger sister. I was so overjoyed at seeing her convalescent that at night I went out, and had a pennyworth of forbidden fruit—a peep into old " Rogers' " show of performing dolls, then exhibiting in the village. When she had begun to take an airing in the " fowt " the doctor gave her his last piece of professional advice.

" All that you want now, Mrs. Brierley, is strength. There is a plant grows in hedge-backings called a September cabbage. This plant is something like the common cabbage, only about the size of a double rose. It is not easily to be found after the early morning, as, unlike other plants, it closes when it begins to feel the warmth of the sun. Get out before six o'clock, and get these cabbages yourself, and boil them an hour, then drink the water when it has cooled. You will find this better than physic."

Morning after morning did my mother obey the doctor's orders, but no " September cabbages " could she find. The doctor happening to call one day, as he often did, to have a chat with my father, he jocularly asked my mother if she had found any benefit from the cabbage water. " Nawe, I ha' not," was the reply. " Perhaps you didn't boil them properly." " I never could find any to boil. I believe, doctor, yo'rn havin' me on." Mister

Esculapius began to chuckle. I can see the fun in his face now as I look back to " auld lang syne." " Esther," he said, addressing my mother, as he sometimes did, by her Christian name, " I don't wonder at you not finding any September cabbages, because there are no such things. I only wanted to get you out into the morning air ; and I can see it has had the desired effect."

About this time satin shawls came into fashion ; and I had the ambition to " tackle " such a high class " reed " of work. I had a loom " gaited " with it,—a 7200, yard and half, quality. In this work I found a silver mine. Whilst weavers of narrow fabrics were earning only ten or twelve shillings per week I was earning my twenty-four ; my father his thirty. Such an income was enough to turn our heads. We seemed to be rolling in wealth ; but it was only for a time. I remember having a warp to " gait," and " twist in " the week before one Whitsuntide, and my father offered me the whole of my earnings for Whissunday brass " if I could complete the half-dozen shawls by the following Thursday. There were only five days, two of which would be required for twisting-in, as I had to do the preliminary work myself, neither " Martin," nor " Dick at Robins " being at liberty. From the first blink of morn to the last gleam of sun-set I was at work, and before breakfast time on Whit-Thursday my scissors had gone across the " tabbing." I had completed my task. My father did the " bearing home ;" and at night handed me the twenty-four shillings that I believe I honestly deserved. Nothing could touch me on the Friday and Saturday. My mother had made me a new " dickey," with half-sleeves to it, like a woman's not-to-be-mentioned. I had a new stuff hat from Mills' at Hollinwood Edge ; old Ned Wray, the Cowhill Cobbler, had brought me a new pair of shoes, and I had my hair, which had been allowed to grow straight down, as some girls wear it now, parted on one side ; and thus rigged out it was—Heigh for Dunham Park, in a boat, on the Saturday.

" Trippers," who go to Blackpool for a day, and take *something* with them, ostensibly to enliven the journey, but which in reality contributes to its dullness, as it generally provokes sleep, know not the luxury of rising by three o'clock in the morning, having a " biting-on " breakfast, and, half awake, setting out for a tramp of five miles, to join an excursion party for a sail on a canal boat. But this was the greatest thing to be done forty years ago. It had to be talked about for weeks before Whit Saturday ; and preparations for the journey were commenced earlier than some people would now think requisite for a voyage across the Atlantic. There was the making and the mending of holiday attire to be done; the—no, not the brewing,—but the baking of extra provisions, such as they were, to be attended to; and other arrangements for the commissariat to be planned. Suitable baskets were not easily attainable; pockets were limited in their holding capacity; and satchels were unknown. The check napkin, the most useful article in a weaver's household, had generally to be resorted to; and it was not a matter of pride to be seen with one under his arm. Gooseberries are not much more than bloom at Whitsuntide; but they have the name of being gooseberries; and that meant something at so early a part of the season. I had a cake of this fruit made for my day's sustenance. It was about the dimensions of a soup plate, and nearly as hard, with not a particle of sugar to sweeten it.

A story is told of a Failsworth youth going to Heaton Park at the time races were held there, and he had an apple cake, made in what was called the "pig" shape, under his arm. On his attempting to enter the park he was stopped by the gate keeper. "We don't allow any *fiddlers* here," said that worthy. "This is no fiddle," said our Failsworth friend; "it's an apple cake." He was allowed to pass after the porter had felt the weight of the supposed fiddle.

A companion of mine now living in Macclesfield was provisioned in a similar way to myself; and thus equipped, with an easterly wind whirling the dust about; and contributing to our comfort in other respects, we set out for Knott Mill wharf at about four o'clock in the morning. The luxury of overcoats had not then begun to make young blood "nesh." We stuck our hands in our pockets; and if they were kept warm the rest of the body had to take care of itself. When we reached Knott Mill a magnificent sight presented itself. There was the boat moored in the basin; and what made our barque specially attractive, the interior was lined with calico; and the planks that had to do for seats were covered with the same material. What was the east wind to us then with such a luxurious furnishing for our roofless saloon? None of us were steerage passengers. What through late comers, and mothers fussing over their children to see to their safety and comfort, it was close upon seven o'clock by the captain's watch when we got "under way." But when the two-horse-power engine warmed to its work the cheering on shore was something to be remembered. How grand to us are things of the past!

Who would stay at home during holiday time?—I had no doubt was everybody's feeling as we entered the arcadia of Dunham Park.

With quite as little doubt I might have said we were sorry for those we had left behind, and wondered if we were being remembered by them. We had strolled over green meadows, but youthful enthusiasm would not have it that the natural carpet we had trod before could be compared to the one that enriched the floor of that vast sylvan cathedral. We had rambled in cloughs where the foliage was thick, and the solitude perfect; but the majesty of the old foresters that were as pillars to the cathedral, and the waving tiles of leaf overhead, excited emotions that only kindle when we see in such works the glory of the Most High.

Coming down to common place things we played at games, some of which were of the simplest kind. Bat and ball had not then made men into boys. The "willow" and the india-rubber, if they were born at all, were in their earliest infancy; and football was the amusement, not the dangerous game of winter. Hunger naturally followed these exercises; and it brought the means of getting rid of our check napkin encumbrances. My companion and I sought a quiet nook; and screened by one of the largest trees we began to devour our gooseberry tarts. There must have been a good deal of face pulling before we had made our full moons into first quarters; and I remember there being allusions made, expressive of longing, to "trayole." Why in our plenitude of pocket wealth had we neglected to provide a pennyworth of sugar?

Well, our habits were so simple, our wants so few, that the idea of becoming extravagant had never before entered our heads. But the money I possessed, the bulk of which I had been persuaded to leave at home, created temptations to indulgences that it is never safe to encourage. My companion even went so far as to wonder what "gradely ale" tasted like. We were familiar with the taste of "smo' drink," which cost about twopence per gallon; but a glass of real "tiger" must be something grand, or people would not sit with it a whole day at once. But, down, temptation! and we crush it. If, however, youths of the present day suffered as much as we did from the effects of eating unripe fruit, the brandy bottle would have to be resorted to. Our return home was conducted with the utmost decorum. The remembrance of it does not remind me of the conduct of pleasure parties such as I have seen since. I was in Blackpool a few years ago, when a day trip had brought hundreds of young people from an adjacent town. I was passing the "tap" corner of the Clifton Arms Hotel about seven o'clock at night, when two young fellows came reeling out of the vault, evidently charged to the muzzle. "Come on, Bill," one says to the other, "it nobbut wants a hauve an' hour to th' train time; an' we ha' no' seen th' sae yet." Such a thing could not have happened with two mere youths forty years ago. They would have spent the day more profitably than in making calls at every public-house they had come near, to the neglect of the chief pleasure that it might be supposed had brought them to the seaside. School boards, and a heavier tax upon racing dogs, may remove some of these evils.

It is now time that my brother entered upon the scene of these "memories." He was three years my junior, and of quite a different disposition. He seemed to be insensible to mental pain. Troubles never annoyed him; and he could look upon a misfortune with almost total unconcern. Things that would have driven me beside myself he regarded with supreme indifference; and yet he was not inconsiderate towards the feelings of others. If a man wept because of his being stricken down by adversity, Tom was willing to admit that he *might* be right, without being able to see the possiblity of it. In fact, we had given him up for making anything except a come-day-go-day youth, who whistled all day, and chased the girls at night, heedless of my father's stick, or my mother's scolding. I remember one winter night sitting with him by the fireside before going to bed, when he showed me a ring. He would then be about thirteen. " Wheere hast had that fro' ? " I asked him. " Jane ——'s gan it me," he replied. " What for ? " " For love, I reckon." My mother, who was plying the bobbin-wheel, overheard our conversation, and turning round, gave the young Lothario one of those mighty slaps that he cared no more about than if it had been the flap of a butterfly's wing. He was always in mischief of some kind, and " wenches " were chiefly at the bottom of it. Many and varied were the articles of prowess that he captured from the fair ones, all of which he showed to me in a boastful spirit. Thirteen times had he been pulled out of the canal before he was so many years of age, and was mixed up with youthful escapades innumerable.

But without becoming sentimental, a change came over his mode of life, and the character of his social pursuits. He had begun to associate with a number of boys who have since made a mark in society. One is now the principal in a cotton manufacturing concern in Ashton-under-Lyne, and is a justice of the peace. Another is his partner; and both are held in high esteem by those who know them. They formed a kind of Mutual Improvement Society among themselves, meeting alternately at each other's homes. I was astonished at the progress my brother made along with his companions. He mastered figures with amazing rapidity, became proficient in phonography, and for a time corresponded with others in a phonetic magazine published by the brothers Pitman. He was a splendid penman; and whilst I was labouring with my cramped hieroglyphics, he could dash off a sentence like the copperplate headings of a copy book. The learning he managed to pick up at this time did him good service in after life. He became " putter-out " in a silk warehouse; but the firm he was employed by failing, he returned to the loom, and followed the occupation of weaving until something better offered.

There are other incentives to a course of life than a liking for it. My brother had been married some years, and had a family growing about him. Weaving only afforded them scant fare, and there was no prospect of its ever being better. Through a little influence he got connected with the Oldham police force, and became his " blue " admirably. He was a fine fellow, about five feet ten, and made in proportion. He was even handsome. He had not long been in the force ere he obtained promotion, being taken from the streets, and put to a clerkship in the police office. In this capacity he died, being taken away by a malignant fever at a time when his prospects appeared to be the brightest. He lies, with his wife and youngest daughter, neither of whom long survived him, in the Chadderton Cemetery. He was so much respected by his brother officers, that his funeral was attended by nearly the whole of the force, led up by the chief constable and his superintendents. My father and mother were both dead; and my feeling was when my brother joined them that, so far as immediate relatives were concerned, I was alone in the world—but this is prospective.

To return to a period when youth begins to think it has got " th' wo'ld in a bant." I had begun to take solitary walks on summer evenings in company with Burns, and Lord Byron. I could recite all the choice passages in " Childe Harold," and repeat all the more popular songs of the gifted ploughman. I was aspiring to be a poet myself, and went so far as to adopt the " Byron tie," and try to look melancholy. The rhyming passion grew upon me; but I have not the courage now to give to the world my first effort. I remember the subject was the death of a " Little Hen." It went through several editions, written, of course, for the edification of my companions, and as a personal tribute to my own vanity. In the study of my favourite authors, I laboured under peculiar disadvantages. I was not allowed a candle during winter nights, so had to read by firelight, until my hair underwent a constant singeing process. I would advise those young men who do not wish to be bald in after years, to deprive themselves of gas and candles during their studies, and poke their heads into the bars of the firegrate, until there is something like the odour of burnt feathers diffused about the hearth. A barber once told me I owed my present hirsute crop to this involuntary singeing in early life. Possibly there may be more truth in the statement than baldheaded people are willing to allow.

My library up to within a few years of this time was exceedingly select. It consisted of penny copies of " Tom Thumb ; " " Jack the Giant Killer ; " " Tummus and Meary " (two vols.) ; " The Adventures of Tom Heckathrift ; " " Chevy Chase ; " " Jack and the Beanstalk ; " " Gulliver's Travels ; " " Kenilworth ; or, Fair Rosamond " (very much condensed) ; " The Lambton Worm ; " and that horrifying story, " The Queer Pack." The rest I have forgotten. The means whereby I was enabled to accumulate this vast store of literary wealth were furnished me by an old pensioner as remuneration for fetching him six cans of water per week a distance of half a mile, a penny being handed to me every Saturday. These funds were augmented by threepence being given to me every pension day for trotting by his side to Manchester and back, and looking after the pocket that he carried his money in. But he always treated me to what was then considered to be a good dinner, and that was something to be remembered after the pinching I had gone through. For such munificence I was exceedingly grateful, and no wonder. The last time I accompanied the old soldier on these errands was on the day of the trial trip on the Manchester and Leeds Railway.

I must confess that my soul did not feel much lifted by the only class of reading then within my reach. It was not until I joined the companionship of Burns and Byron that I felt the " god within me." Music followed, or was the attendant on poetry ; and nightly I charmed the ear, or thought I did, with the tones of an accordion. I very soon learned to play the instrument to my own satisfaction, if not to that of others. But one night I had been out serenading the moon, and the deities that haunted the woods, when a storm came on. I took shelter in a cottage where a fiddle hung in the nook. Here, I thought, was an opportunity of paying for the hospitality I was enjoying, besides my music being thoroughly appreciated. Accordingly, I struck up " There is nae luck," but before I had got through many bars I was told by the head of the family that "he had a cauve could gie better music than that."

Thus was a musical genius annihilated at once by the adventitious criticism of a fiddling old farmer. I gave up Orpheus, and stuck to the "tuneful nine." But I began to feel that I was deficient in figures, as younger boys could outstrip me. I had the knowledge that only required rubbing up, consequent on my neglect of them whilst mooning with the muses. My next-door neighbour, a married man, felt the want of a knowledge of arithmetic, through weaving a class of work that required a good deal of calculation. We agreed to exercise by our two selves. I was to lead the way from addition onwards, and very closely he followed me. It was from spring to autumn when these schoolings took place. Up by five o'clock every morning, except Sundays, we pegged at it until seven, when we took to our looms. Those were long days, as we did not give up weaving until nearly dusk. Then to our summer recreations—not cricket, nor lacrosse, but toiling in the garden until the last note of the throstle piped the close of day. My schoolmate was the man of whom I related the following anecdote in a speech I delivered during the last parliamentary election:—

"When a boy I remember a neighbour telling my mother that his wife was heating the oven. Being at the beginning of the week my mother was surprised. What, baking so early? No, it was washing day, and his second shirt was so thick with layers of patches that it was impossible to dry it by ordinary means; so it had to be baked."

To the curious it might be interesting to note the fashions that were in vogue forty years ago. I do not know if the Parisians led the taste in such matters as they do at the present time; if they did, their influence was confined to the aristocracy. The working classes did not share it. If my mother was to pass down Market Street attired in her cloak and bonnet of the time, the Sultan of Zanzibar could not have created a greater attraction. Those of our readers who have seen pictorial illustrations of the mouth of the Mersey Tunnel will get some idea from it of the perspective of the interior of that bonnet. It was of extraordinary dimensions even for the period. I can only remember her wearing it on one occasion, and that was when she went to the Primitive Methodists' Chapel, to hear a lady "local," Mary Crossley, preach. After the sermon Mary left the pulpit, and singling out my mother from the rest of the congregation, dropped on her knees beside her, and prayed that she might be delivered from the sins of worldly pride.

c

The bonnet was at once consigned to its oval-shaped box, where it has remained ever since, being kept as a curiosity by a surviving relative. Of the crimson cloaks there are none now worn, but I remember a time when a funeral procession resembled at a distance a troop of soldiers, from the presence of these cloaks. But it was only on extraordinary occasions that bonnets and cloaks were worn. It was more common, even on Sundays, for women to be considered "dressed" when, with a silk handkerchief tied over a white cap, and a "napkin-shawl" of the same material pinned over the shoulder, they enlivened the lanes and by-paths on fine summer evenings by their showiness.

An amusing instance of this want of distinction betwixt Sunday and work-a-day dress occurs to my recollection. Two grown-up girls, companions, met on a Sunday morning. The weather was temptingly fine. "Hannah," said the one to the other, "goo an' get thysel' wesht, an' let's goo deawn th' cutside." "Wesht," as applied, meant washed and dressed. "I am wesht," said Hannah, with tears in her eyes. Poor girl! she had nothing to change on, and consequently felt her position. What would our "masher-esses" of the present day think of such times?

Boots were not worn by women except in isolated instances. The well-to-do matron might encase her feet in "stuff" shoes, protected from universal mud by "ringed pattens," but the weaver girl had to be satisfied with a pair of well-polished clogs, of which the bright brass buckles formed no mean part of the adornment. Well, these had their attractiveness; and when a strip of white lambs-wool stocking could be seen above the instep, and a pair of rosy cheeks, and eyes sparkling with witchery, were not concealed beneath a cascade of hair, but had their brightness set off by the flowing silk handkerchief, it was odds on some lad's heart becoming bothered.

I wonder what would now be thought of the "swell" or "masher" of that period. Whenever I see a child's toy representing a monkey on a stick I am reminded of him. A swallow-tailed coat, with the skirts extraordinarily narrow, a pair of tightly-fitting sleeves, through which plenty of wrist was visible; trousers equally tight in the legs, and held down over the calf by straps, to which irreverent boys gave the name of "linderins" (weavers' lengthening strings), a tie that would have done for a double sema-phore, a penny cane, and a hat, if he could afford one, completed the attire of the "lady-killer" of forty years ago. Were he now to pass through St. Ann's Square at "fashion's hour" people would expect to see his "keeper" not far away.

Aspiring to know more than could be taught me at the Sunday School in Hollinwood, I joined the one known as the "Old School," in Pole Lane, Failsworth. I was at home again, in the very room where a dozen years before I was taught the alphabet. Here I found a number of congenial spirits, who, like myself, had grown out of their childhood, and were looking forward to becoming men. We banded ourselves together, and formed the nucleus of the present Mechanics' Institution, then existing under the name of the Mutual Improvement Society. Wonders were to be done by this body of aspirants to learned greatness; and some of them were accomplished. Never was more delightful work engaged in than in the earlier struggles of this Society. We desked round the small room we had set aside for our exclusive use; and did other carpentry jobbing in quite a workman-like manner. I remember one evening whilst we were engaged in this great undertaking we fell short of a kind of material indispensable to building purposes. In this emergency our chairman (*pro. tem.*) called us together, and said—"Will anybody *dominer* to go to Jim Blunderick's for a penno'th o' nails?" We knew not then that he had made a "blunder." Like newly-married people who look forward to important events we made our cradle before the child was born— we shelved a corner to accommodate what we had the presumption to call a library. But we had no books, nor had we yet the means of purchasing any. I remember the late Elijah Ridings once saying to me—"If I'd fifty pounds I'd go to Lunnon, an' buy a ton o' books;" what a magnificent spectacle that presented to me!

Supplies came at last, we had been subscribing our pennies weekly until the sum had amounted to something worthy of being invested in literature, and this was to be spent. My uncle, Richard Taylor, who lived near to the School, and was taking an active interest in our Society, was appointed to select a number of volumes from some of the old bookshops in Manchester. He had been a great reader, and was well up in not only literature but some of the sciences, so that we could depend upon the choice he would make. I was one of two youngsters told off to carry the books when bought, and were we not proud of the appointment? Elated at the idea of seeing our empty shelves stocked we set out one Saturday afternoon to meet my uncle, who was employed in Manchester, taking with us a weavers' wallet in which to carry the books. The necessary purchases were made; our wallet filled until the weight of it made us stagger; but there being no other means of conveyance in those days, we had to struggle with it until we boarded the treasure in its proper place. It afterwards became a labour of love to cover the bindings, which we did with stout nankeen, so as to make them last for ever. This work accomplished we had a show night for friends, who, while they encouraged us in our undertaking, did not think we could have achieved so much in so short a time. From that nucleus our "library" grew until the shelves could no longer accommodate it; so we had an elegant bookcase made by a professional joiner, doing the painting and varnishing ourselves. I can see in memory the daub we made of that work. But it was a grand cabinet to us, and caused us to wonder if Manchester possessed anything like it.

The Saturday evening meetings in our little room were some of the most delightful I ever spent. Billiard tables were unknown; and as there were no incentives to drinking, we could disperse to our homes without a brawl, but not before we had planned a walk to some one of the districts outside, as on Saturday nights we were not expected to go to bed so early as we did on other nights. Some of these peregrinations extended over miles. I remember on one occasion we did not turn back until we had crossed the border into Yorkshire, going by way of Oldham and Lees to Saddleworth. In these walks we enlivened the way by discoursing upon our favourite books, upon problems in arithmetic, and new kinds of weaving. The too common frivolities of youth we avoided. From the seeds sown at this time harvests have been gathered. The Crossley Brothers, manufacturers and machinists, sprung from amongst us. Others are successful farmers in America; and one is a partner in a firm of auctioneers in San Francisco. Of the boys connected with my class in the Sunday school, one occupies a good position in a manufacturing concern at Pendleton. Another is a large employer of labour in Ashton, and an occupant of the judicial bench. And now I cannot refrain from publishing a letter I recently received from a friend and old acquaintance, now resident in one of our more northern counties. He was not one of our band, but although attending another school, I had opportunities of knowing that we had his sympathies in the severest struggles we had afterwards, and for years, to face. My friend writes—

Registrar's Office, Staindrop,
26th March, 1884.

My dear Ben,—I know not—but I cannot—I *know not* whether in the midst of your present excitement and pressing anxieties you will have time to peruse a communication from an old acquaintance, but I *cannot* let the opportunity pass without expressing my most heartfelt sympathy for you in any troubles which may have over-taken you, and my earnest hope that your contemplated visit to our cousins in America may gratify your every wish, and be conducive to your happiness and comfort in your declining years.

It is highly gratifying to see your friends and the public rallying around you at this crisis, as it demonstrates forcibly that your high abilities and the toil you have gone through to amuse and instruct are duly appreciated.

Oh! Ben! Reminiscences connected with your career are passing vividly, and like flashes of lightning through my mind. Coming as I did, 40 years ago next June, to Failsworth, a mere stripling in a round jacket, I had an opportunity of watching silently your poetical budding—the sturdy struggle about the old school—your song on that occasion, the Manchester trial, &c., and further on, I remember the meeting of the "literati," at old John Pollitt's, the "Philo," where I had the honour of being a very nervous chair-man in the presence of the brilliancy and wit of old Sam Bamford, Bolton Rogerson, yourself, and others, and still further on, the many sallies of humour and wit, in which you and Will Crossley indulged, at his residence in Dob Lane, and which were listened to with gusto and delight by the most lamented and dearest friend I ever had, James Hall, and myself. Nay, nay, I might go on but am afraid of being tedious. Something dimly tells me that Will, too, is gone—I hope not.

I have a lively recollection of my entrance into Failsworth. Many changes will have taken place since then, but there will be many left who will remember that event.

Memories incidental to the life of a schoolmaster will still be cherished of me in Failsworth—It was there I budded into man-hood—loved—married and made myself a family man—It was there I spent the happiest days of my life, though clouded and blackened with many trials and troubles. There I have long hoped—but I am afraid the hope is a forlorn one—that I might spend, along with my wife, the remainder of our days, and be buried close to the church in the ceremony of the laying of the foundation of which I played a humble but conspicuous part.

Would you kindly tell any of my old friends who may be desirous to know that I live with my wife alone, in a pretty cottage, in a pretty little town close to Raby Castle, the largest inhabited one in England, except Windsor, that my health is excellent, my brain and sight clear, my heart beats with a right pulsation, and my lungs are more powerful than ever—weigh 15 stone—am sober and temperate, and that I am growing a jolly old man.

Tell them that my duties in my present situation demand that I should keep a watchful eye on the progressive increase in the population—enter the names of the new comers into the National Register—cause them to undergo a surgical operation to prevent the spread of a loathsome disease—watch over them as they advance to maturity—relieve them, if in distress, and not one of them can be laid low after their exit, without my special sign manual.

I am Registrar of Births and Deaths—Vaccinating Officer and Relieving Officer for the District of Staindrop, comprising fifteen townships in the counties of Durham and York and Union of Teesdale.

Remember me kindly to your good wife— by the bye—our lamented friend James Hall told me a characteristic story of her in our younger days—" James, she said to him one day—our Ben goes to this party and that party neglecting his wark, giving his readings and what not, and there's so much paid at th' dur, but I never see any o'th' brass. But I'll go and be th' dur keeper and then !—that I will ! "

Now, Ben, if your fingers are as slippery as mine, let her take care o'th' brass during your American tour, and may be there'll be a bit of sticking plaster at th' end of her fingers.

Again wishing you every success,

I am, faithfully yours,

THOMAS HOUGH.

P.S.—Mrs. Hough desires to be remembered to you and yours.

T. H.

Having established our " Mutual Improvement Society," we took a further departure from Sunday Schools conducted on ordinary lines. We had begun a few of us to assemble early on Sabbath mornings in the summer in " My Uncle's Garden," and had read to us passages from Shakespeare, Shelley, Burns, and Byron. These exercises imbued us with a love of reading, especially poetry. I had from my early youth been " stage-struck." I had been accustomed to going to Oldham whenever I could get hold of a penny, to patronise " Williamson's Theatre." which used to be pitched for months together in " Tommy Fielt." I knew and worshipped most of the stars that shone in that firmament. I had had the honour of shaking hands with " Bill Evans." I had touched the hem of " Jack Lyons' " garment when

he swept the outside platform in the majestic robes of an emperor.
I had had one ear patronised by the finger and thumb of " Tom
Mellor," the greatest clown of his day (I thought), when he
wanted to look down my throat, to see if I had swallowed his
slipper. But these honours were bought at a certain cost. The
last time I visited this " Temple of Thespis," my father caught me
coming out. He patronised me for a time; but neither his fist,
nor his foot, could cure me of my love for the " drawmar."
Events will show how this passion haunted me in after life. I
paid stealthy visits to Tommy Fielt to be an outside spectator, but
never durst venture up the ladder, for fear I might be again caught;
so spent my penny on " duck an' mouffin."

Those of us who frequented my uncle's garden were kindred
spirits. They, too, had a love for theatricals, and after witnessing
such glories as could be obtained for a penny, wondered what
could be seen at a legitimate establishment. Our ambition to see
Shakespeare in real gold and silk and feathers was a feeling to be
gratified, and we determined that it should be. When we had
mustered so much " brass " as would get us admittance to the
gallery of the old Theatre Royal in Fountain-street, Manchester,
we took the earliest opportunity of making acquaintance with some
of the finest actors of the time. The wonders that were held out
to us as if by the hand of some mighty magician after we had
elbowed our way to the heights of the gallery, were enough to
strike us with awe. The band was not like one we had been
accustomed to hear, that could play nothing but " Old Billy," and
an air from Norma ; but something to carry us away to " Where
Orpheus tuned his lyre," and Apollo " tootled " to the gods on
Mount Parnassus. But when the curtain rose, and disclosed the
witches' scene in " Macbeth," the sight made me feel as though I
had only had the experience of a baby. John Reeve, now Sims
Reeves, was in this cast ; Pitt and Butler were the principals, and
Miss Emiline Montague was Lady Macbeth. The rest of the
performers were all " made to match," and the way in which the
play went was a treat to be remembered for a lifetime. When we
returned home, we were all of us Macbeths and Macduffs, and no
doubt we made " night hideous " with our spoutings, if we only
could have appreciated them at their proper worth.

The result of our first acquaintance with the legitimate stage led
us to aspire to be specks of light in the milkyway about which the
constellations revolved. We had done " spangles " along with
other boys to adorn with grand pictures the walls of our humble

homes. I had loaded " St. David of Wales " with a shield that hid nearly the whole of his body, and a pair of spurs that would have done for children's wheelbarrows. I had given a sword to the " Earl of Richmond " that in its proportionate dimensions would have made a saw for a giant. Osbaldiston and O'Smith, as pirates and smugglers, I had clothed with tunics of red and blue satin ; and the skirt of Mrs. Honey, as the Fairy Queen, I had adorned with silver butterflies. Malibran's robe was too long and too costly for me, so I stuck to " dots " and short petticoats. But to become one of these figures, and be " spanked " like them, was a dream of the future never to be realised. If, however, we could not be gods, we might, perhaps, attain the distinction of godlings.

We set about at once and planned a stage. Rude and meagre were the materials out of which we proposed to do honour to the histrionic art. A number of planks that served as a gallery for the choir at " Charities " and Christmas " peace speakings," were appropriated to our use ; and in the absence of scenery, we had a pair of green bed-quilts strung across the stage. An orchestra composed of a flute, a clarionet, and a bassoon, played the " Overture," which had been arranged out of a dovetailing of several hymn tunes. Our first piece was " Ducks and Peas ; or, the Newcastle Rider," a little behind Shakespeare, but good enough for a start. I played (with) " Joseph," which brought down the advice of my mother, not to be " too consequential."

The success of our first attempt at acting led us to try another rung on fame's ladder. This was Christmas ; and the interval betwixt then and Easter would afford us time to cook something bigger than " Ducks and Peas." The ambition of a Bonaparte fired my breast,—I would write the piece; and set about the work with as much assurance as if I had written all Shakespeare's plays, and allowed him for a consideration to claim the authorship. In a few days, during which my father thought the loom was rather silent, as I did not weave in the same room as he worked in, I produced a terrible tragedy under the title of " Marinello the Monk ; or, the Italian Lovers." With what a shout of approval it was welcomed ! Every character was a " part ; " so that there was no murmuring at the cast. There were daggers to be used in the piece,—two tin ones, costing threehalfpence each, and a veritable pistol,—an old flint that sometimes would not " go off " when murder was to be committed, but create a scare when it was not in the plot. Being the author, I had the privilege assigned to me of taking the leading part,—the villain of the piece. Almost smothered beneath the folds of a black cloak belonging to an aunt, I stalked about the stage—planks, I mean—intent upon my murderous design, in a manner that I have imagined since, Irving must have copied, it was so melodramatic. To give *eclat* to the proceedings, we had a tea party to begin with, the first ever held in Failsworth; and the tables in the bottom room were crowded with three relays of "tea-fighters." A home-made balloon, the shape of a kidney potatoe, was sent up, accompanied by a *feu de joie* of three guns to notify to the public that the doors were open.

When the performance was over, all who had taken part in it were lionized, excepting myself, who had created such a dislike that my little sweetheart declared she would have nothing more to say to "sich a bad un as thee." That cured me of dramatic authorship for a very long time. If I am suffering from a severe cold, and wish to sweat it away, I think of that attempt to become great; and perspiration requires no additional stimulants to make it boil out of me.

From that time we had a tea party and a dramatic performance every Easter Monday for years. Southey's "Wat Tyler" was our first ambitious effort. After that "William Tell." Only fancy two armies meeting, fighting, and subverting a government, on three or four planks; and you will think less of the glories of the battlefield, and the dignities of rulers. We grew in our own estimation, until "Othello" was not too big an undertaking for us. That was a memorable performance. A blacker "Moor" never trod the stage than the one we selected to murder "Desdemona," and himself as well, let alone Shakespeare. We knew not then of the application of burnt cork. Our only source of swarthy pigment was the house chimney, which was pretty well swept before "Othello's occupation" began. We smeared the Moor's face until his eyes resembled a couple of pigeon's eggs set in ebony. The colour was "fixed" by requisitions we made on a candle box, which gave the glossiness of satin to the dusky general's face. A pair of funeral gloves, warranted to fit any size of hand, dangled from his digits; and with my uncle's frock coat, tied round the waist with a red worsted "comfortor," Othello was ready to appear before the "Duke."

I was cast for "Iago." Well do I remember the dressing for that great part, and the shifts I was put to to obtain suitable articles of costumery. I could not afford to be otherwise than showy, to act as a foil to Othello; so I ransacked Smithfield Market to find a soldier's cast-off coat; but not being able to obtain one, I had to put up with a shell jacket minus buttons. For this splendid garment I paid the magnificent sum of tenpence; but discovered afterwards, to my dismay, that I had purchased more than I bargained for. The thing had to be subjected to severe measures of quarantine before it received its supply of buttons. But the enemy was slain at last. A pair of white trousers, borrowed from a member of the Hollinwood Band, made rather slack substitutes for tights, as they had to be turned up at the bottom to prevent their sweeping the stage. Had we known such a kind of fowl at the time, it might have been said that I resembled a " Cochin China," with a red back. My neck was encircled by a girl's lace tippet which covered my shoulders, and folded gracefully about my buttons. My hat had a bonnet feather stuck on one side; and it has never been a settled question with me whether the design for the headgear of *Punch's* dog was not suggested by my appearance on that occasion. Thus " made up," it would have been impossible to suspect that I had the slightest idea of villainy; or that I had the craftiness to lure the black fly into my fatal web. Of the performance it would be kindness to say nothing; but one little incident I cannot forget. I was standing at the wing supporting Desdemona's head in the smothering scene, when I overheard a few words that were not in the text, nor in the stage directions. Othello was just saying—

> " Put out the light, and then put out the light ;
> If I quench thee, thou flaming minister,
> I can again thy former light restore;
> Should I repent me ;—but once put out thine,
> Thou cunning'st pattern of excelling nature,
> I know not where is the Promethean heat,
> That can thy light relume. When I have pluck'd thy rose,
> I cannot give it vital breath again,
> It needs must wither ; I'll smell it on the tree.

When Othello was stooping to obtain the coveted kiss, I overheard Desdemona saying to him, " C——, thou munno' buss me gradely, thou'll sooty my nose."

We afterwards played " The Stranger ; " " Virginius ; " " The Lear of Private Life ; " Black-eyed Susan ; " and " Douglas." In the latter, I took the part of Glenalvon, and smashed a tenpenny sword, much to the alarm of the audience, amongst whom one of the pieces flew. Alas, we are now a scattered " troupe." " Young Norval " is in America, where I hope to see him in a few weeks hence ; " Othello " is in London ; and " Susan," " William," and " Bullfrog " are in the grave.

These dramatic performances excited the jealousy of the young people connected with the neighbouring school. Every Easter Sunday the officiating clergyman preached against them as being iniquitous; and it was believed at the time that he was the means of inducing a gentleman who held a prominent position in the township to take measures for closing the school. Belonging to the ratepayers the building had no trusteeship; but was held for the time being by the schoolmaster then in possession. Our schoolmaster died; then war was declared, and carried out to the bitter end.

The school was entered from the school-house by a gang of men, the door of the bottom room fastened by strong iron bars; but for want of foresight they had neglected to secure the door of the upper room first; and we held the key of the front door. We put a man in possession at once, and secured nine points of the law in that respect. Both day school and Sunday school were carried on in the upper room, the schoolmaster for the time occupying the " Garret," in which our young Mechanic's Institution was held. Rioting and rowdyism became rampant; and seldom a week passed over without a batch of " physickites," as we were termed, having to appear at the New Bailey.

One Saturday night we had a " forlorn hope " organised. We were determined upon obtaining access to the bottom room of the school. We entered the school at the usual hour for night teaching; but not with the purpose of consulting either Bonnycastle, or Lindley Murray. We were as well furnished with tools for house-breaking as would have given a professional burglar the heartache. It being summer time, we stretched ourselves on the forms for a make-believe sleep; and at break of day we went to work. A square hole was made in the floor; and there being no ceiling, it was an easy matter to get through. One by one, three of us were let down into the bottom school. I held the door communicating with the school-house, and had the satisfaction of hearing the watchman snoring, whilst a companion permanently secured the door with a rope. Whilst this was doing, the third party was quietly removing the bars from the entrance door, which was but the work of a few minutes. Our object was accomplished; and at ten o'clock the school was in full swing.

The surprise of our opponents upon hearing the hum of school life in the bottom room was both interesting and amusing. As the entrance made had been the work of nobody, no one was the wiser, and we had sufficient caution to keep the secret.

After this incident our persecution took another form. I was accused of writing a *jeu d' esprit*, in which two of our opponents' leaders were lampooned. They could not prove authorship against me; but I was dogged by spies until I was caught disposing of a copy. An action for libel in the Court of Queen's Bench was at once entered against me; and I was served with a writ in due course. A declaration was filed, which had to be met. I had R. B. B. Cobbett, and Sergeant Wilkins against me; and matters looked rather serious. I cannot now call to mind the name of *our* Counsel, only we had Mr. James Heron, brother to Sir Joseph, for our solicitor; and it was confidently expressed that the case would never go into court, or that the plaintiffs would not obtain a verdict. The case did go into court, but an apology, which neither I nor my friends were personal to, was accepted, and the action was withdrawn. This ended a very troublesome time.

And now I am reminded of a remarkable, if not a romantic, experience in a not uneventful career. At the time the Old School at Failsworth was held by our opponents, a few of us migrated to Hollinwood, where we established the nucleus of a Mechanics' Institute. Here I became acquainted with a young man of rather reserved habits, who was book-keeper at a mill. He had formed no companionship with anyone, nor did he seem to seek any. He had the name of being a great reader, but of a class of literature that was as yet beyond our reach—the works of Goethe, Schiller, and the expounders of what is known as " German philosophy." I had a desire to become more intimately acquainted with this young man, and as the will led, the way was found. He proved to be of quite a different disposition to what we had taken him to be after the ice had been broken. There can be no doubt that a peculiar bodily deformity induced his shyness, which once cast aside revealed a gem of a fellow behind it. We became strongly attached to each other, and spent many happy evenings together. My friend lodged with an old woman and her daughter opposite the Pole at Failsworth, and here I used to call frequently. His conversation charmed me. It was in every sense a new light to me. I lived in another world than the one I was supposed to inhabit. Belonging to the Unitarian body, he had a mentor in Mr. Poynting, the minister at Monton Green, near Eccles, travelling every Sunday the distance between the two places, to listen to the ministrations of that worthy gentleman.

My father took favourably to this young man; and he and my mother allowed me certain indulgences on his account. Being a book-keeper he was looked upon as belonging to a higher class of society than ours. Whenever he visited me, which was generally on Saturday evenings, we were allowed a cloth on the table; and my mother even went so far as to purchase a pair of steel snuffers and a brass tray, to give the table an aristocratic appearance. A pair of old scissors had been used for snuffers before. Verily, we were looking up in the world.

But an event occurred that tended very much to interfere with our symposium. One evening there came a knock to the door at the house where my friend lodged. On being answered, two young ladies stepped in. Strangers they were, seeking lodgings. Both were remarkably prepossessing, yet not by any means alike. One was a soft blue-eyed blonde; the other was a brunette, and had a dash about her that appeared at first to be somewhat stagy. I have seen a portrait of Eliza Cook in her younger days. That portrait, with the curls, and the facial expression, the young lady under notice might have sat for. Being of respectable appearance, and showing no lack of means, they were accommodated with lodgings. Strange!—they had come to work at the very mill my friend was book-keeper at. But they were no mill workers. Common gossip said they were something else; but from their behaviour, and their constantly being either at the mill or at home, there was no reason to suppose they were other than respectable girls, possibly runaways from a boarding school, or to escape from some kind of persecution. They were taught the business of "reeling," and for a time they appeared to be happy with their work, and contented with their home. But at times I could observe a cloud steal over the face of the darker one, and there was fire in her piercing black eyes.

I never could divine the mystery that was hidden behind those looks. They were only transient, and might have been the result of a species of insanity. When the light storm had passed over she would resume her cheerful demeanour, and appear as if nothing had interfered with it. But there was a weight of woe that had to be accounted for some way. Once the old landlady caught her in tears, when she poured out her grief as though her heart would break.

But she never hinted at any cause. The two girls did not, so far as we knew, correspond with anybody, but kept the secret of their lives as profoundly as if they had nothing to divulge or conceal. Time went on in the same uninteresting way that distinguishes suburban from urban life, until a communication was received that caused a sensation in our little circle. From the receipt of that communication things assumed a new phase. The girls intimated that they were about to leave us, and without saying whither they were going, or what was the cause of their sudden departure, they left Failsworth one Monday morning, after paying what they owed, and taking an affectionate leave of their friends. From one of them I constructed the character of "Ellen Moreton," in my story "Cast upon the World," which is partly autobiographical.

Of all the pastimes held in Hollinwood the "Wakes" was the crowning event; but the rushcart was discontinued, or was only brought out at long intervals. I cannot remember more than two. One was so much of a failure that the inscription on the back of the cart was a characteristic apology for the whole affair:—"No GRUMBLING." Not an ounce of silver was displayed on the sheet, which was all the prettier from the garlands and bouquets of flowers it contained. But the *value* was not there, and that was considered everything. After an interval of several years, the second, and final effort to resuscitate the pageant was a great success. Sixteen couples of morris dancers led up the cart, and these were specially attired. They were not merely decorated with ribbons, but each dancer wore a pair of coloured breeches, made for the occasion, one rank blue, the other red; which had a peculiar effect when "crossing morris." The stocking continuations were white; and where one of the troop had not grown his calves they were substituted with false ones, not very artistically made, nor were they warranted to keep their place. They were right enough on setting out, but when the day's dancing was finished they presented a ludicrous appearance. One of these fellows provoked the remark—"Bill, theau's getten thy legs on th' wrong end up." The calves had worked down to his ankles. The whole thing cost so much money that no further attempt at a revival was ever made. From that time the wakes gradually fell into the hands of showmen, steam driven horses, nut stalls, and "hit-my-legs-and-miss-my-pegs." As an annual festivity it is now nothing.

But there were pastimes quite as enjoyable for the time as the wakes. There was the annual bonfire on the fifth of November. This was a great institution. Being held in the vicinity of a number of collieries, the young people had facilities for obtaining combustibles that were out of the reach of others. One fire I remember to have consumed twenty loads of an inferior kind of coal, which was called "boson," and cost about twopence per waggon. The pile was a monster, and lasted over three days, during which time the firing of " pop guns " never ceased, night or day.

Then there was the annual "pig-washing," which afforded a couple of hours' roaring fun. On the second of May the Oldham Spring Fair was held. Droves of pigs were driven from Manchester, and these were washed in the basin of the Peak Forest Canal. After being soaped and scrubbed in the shallower part of the basin they were taken to the deeper part near the bridge, and there soused into the water. But the pigs were not the only animals that had to contend with the element. There were others, with white aprons, and cord trousers, had sometimes to share the dip. Then was the time when the fun came in. In a locality that was only a nook of Hollinwood there was a lot of character to be found : notably, Fred Kearsley, one of the cripples I made acquaintance with the night we removed from Failsworth. Then there was the other cripple who was weaving at the time. Both of these were assisted in their perambulations by an arm crutch and a stick. The spectators of the pig washings would not have been the usual muster without these two. They seemed to court disaster, for no sooner did they present themselves on the scene than it was a signal for a general " skiver." There would be a " school" of variously clothed porpoises floundering in the water at once, crutches and sticks playing a prominent part. I have seen Fred Kearsley pushed in three times at one washing. But he enjoyed it.

Fred, I remember well. He used to go about " twisting-in " for hand-loom weavers. But it was surprising to see how he could buckle to the loom. It was as good as a pantomime to watch him weave. The various wriggling motions his body went through at every " pick-o'er," would have been painful to see, had he not been himself conscious of the ludicrous figure he made, and laughed with others. But with all these physical draw-backs, Fred had the reputation of being one of the wealthiest of his class, and often lent money to those who were more able than he to earn it.

There was an unmarried woman living with her brother at one corner of " Muffin Row," who wove a coarse kind of work to which the name of " thin goods " was given. On one occasion Fred was called in to assist in the " beaming," or, as it was then called, " winding on," a fresh warp. This had to be done previous to his being employed in the " twisting-in." In those days a house could not be built, or any other kind of out-door work be undertaken, without a number of spectators superintending, and advising in the work. There was a stout joiner who wished to fill up an hour or two's holiday time, who was directing in his way, the winding-on of his neighbour's "piece;" when suddenly he seized hold of Fred's arm crutch, slipped it under the "ratch," and before Fred had a chance of recovering it, his principal bodily stay was wound on to the beam, where it had to remain until it was woven off. The poor fellow had to "haumple" about a whole fortnight with a stick, it taking that time to weave off the crutch. Well, in those days the only fun people had was in practical joking. If we were to attempt to do the things now-a-days that were done then, the police would be called in, and a journey to Manchester have to be performed.

The stout joiner was the father of many a good practical joke, which originated in an eccentric turn of mind. They were not jokes that anyone else would be likely to think of. One quite as remarkable as the winding-on affair he played upon his wife. It happened to be a fine summer Sunday afternoon, when no one cared to be indoors. The joiner's wife had arranged with several other neighbour women to go " a-walking " by Birchen Bower, which was a favourite haunt at holiday times. The husbands had to be left at home whenever these " hen " outings took place, as the wives did not care for their company. "Betty," like a cautious housewife, entreated her husband not to leave the door in her absence, not that she was afraid of thieves, but there was no telling what might happen. "Now, then, whatever thou does, dunno' *leeave th' dur*," was her last injunction. The husband promised he would not. But the afternoon was too temptingly fine for him. He kept going to the door, and looking up at the blue sky, which seen from a dingy *cul de sac* was rendered more beautiful by the contrast, until at length the temptation became too strong for him. An idea struck him, which he proceeded at once to put into effect. The post-office corner, with its stumps and railings, was always a resort for those who had an idle hour to spend, and wished to see what was passing. It was the " gossip exchange," if I may use the term. "Betty," on returning from her walk, had to pass this corner, and what was her astonishment to find her husband there, with the *house door* set up against the railings! He had promised not to *leave* it, and had kept his word. He had lifted the door off its "angles," and, like Samson with the gates of Gaza, borne it on his back through the streets to the highway. The only intruders in the house during the absence of the door were a couple of hens, that were found perching on the back of a chair.

Whoever may claim to be the inventor of the " screw propeller," I claim for Mr. John Taylor, then a young gentleman of Hollinwood, to be the first to test its adaptability to canal navigation. He and his father were proprietors of a rope and twine manufactory at Birchen Bower, and a slate wharf on the canal. The young man had quite a genius for mechanical inventions, and I believe among his greatest achievements was the construction of a model screw steamer which was to ply on the canal. It was built and fitted in the slate wharf. " There's many a slip betwixt the cup and the lip," is a trite adage ; and there was a " slip " connected with the fortunes of this model steam-boat that is not yet forgotten. The day for launching was announced, and when that day came all Bradley Bent was a-stir. The gates of the wharf were thrown open, and everybody was permitted to inspect the novel craft. My father was one of the privileged few, obtained through influence, who were allowed on board during the launch. The cabin was battened, as a precaution against accidents, and the privileged few took their stand on the fore-deck. I forget whether a bottle of wine was broken against the hull, or that a name was given to the boat; but it had a thorough *christening* for all that, and the sponsors were very much in earnest during one part of the ceremony. The signal was given to " let go," and it went. But the gradient of the incline had not been taken into account, and was too steep for the purpose, hence a scene that reminded me of a " pig-washing." The boat must have mistaken itself for a duck, as it sent its prow right under the water, leaving its living freight floundering in the same element, like so many pigs. There were shouts of—not alarm—but laughter from the " shore " at this mishap, but the vessel righted itself after its bath, and floated bravely. It was not, however, allowed to ply on the canal, owing to the " wash " damaging the banks, which were only of earth.

My connection with the Failsworth Mechanics' Institution led to the forming of other connections which have since proved valuable to me. There were societies like ours springing up around us, and with which we were to a certain extent affiliated. On the bursting up of the Chartist movement the branch association held at Pew Nook, Hollinwood, threw aside its politics, and the members turned their attention to intellectual pursuits. We had many a pleasant reunion at this place, and although our means were limited we got a better return in enjoyment than is obtained in these days. Our pleasures were simple and quiet, not expensive and exciting; we were as pleased to hear a white-aproned matron warble

D

"Highland Mary" as we should be now by listening to Patti's aerial flights of song. No billiards, no cards, left us time to read; and as smoking was not practised except by elderly people and "swells," we were never in an atmosphere rendered offensive by the fumes of "thick twist" or cabbage leaf. We did occasionally indulge in a dance, those of us who knew how, and from what I can remember this dancing was no sleepy or shuffling affair, but a good hearty flinging up of heels. No suggestive hugging was tolerated, and he who ventured upon this objectionable practice was as likely to get a slap as not. Had the room been larger, no doubt, it would have afforded a better display of feminine grace and masculine abandonment, but being no larger than a four-loomed loomhouse, the dancers were "all amang." But "poor men's houses" had to do for chapels in those days, as well as for other institutions. There was no putting up of large buildings without a farthing to begin with.

Another of these societies existed at "Nimble Nook," in Chadderton. This also was held in a cottage house. Men who have since made their way in the world "graduated" at this modest "university." There was another held in a cottage at "Jumbo," near Middleton; one at Cow Hill, in Chadderton; and another in Maygate Lane, near Oldham, all of which were doing good work among the young men who attended—the fathers and grandfathers of the present day. The last I remember of these happy acquaintances was formed at the top of Hollinwood, a district mostly inhabited by colliers. Here it was my pleasure to witness one Sunday morning early the assembling of a number of young men, some of them bearing the trade mark of a miner—the blue scars on the face, not for the getting up of a "pigeon-fly" or a wrestling match, but for mutual instruction; the leading spirit of that little colony being my old friend James Dronsfield ("Jerry Lichenmoss"), a man of inestimable qualities as a man, and as a writer full of the quaintest humour, added to good common sense. Many a droll story of his has appeared from time to time in the *Oldham Chronicle*, and I am not sure that I have not myself gathered inspiration from being in his society.

While the events named in the last few pages were passing, changes were going on at home. I was growing into manhood, and nourishing the ambitious thoughts that make youth restless at that important period of life. I had a strong desire to be employed in Manchester, and join Manchester society. My uncle in Failsworth had been employed there for years as a silk warper, and he was the means of getting room made for me in the warehouse belonging to Messrs. J. T. and T. Walker, Silk Manufacturers, York Street, the manager of which concern was a younger uncle. This change was as a new existence to me—not the most pleasant at first, having to learn the business, and to walk four and a half miles to my work in the early morning, and the same distance home after seven at night, there being no 'buses at the time plying betwixt Hollinwood and Manchester. I entered upon my new duties the day following the public rejoicings on the occasion of the repeal of the Corn Laws. During the same month other rejoicings took place in honour of the opening of the Public Parks; and I was so impressed with these stirring events that I thought Manchester life was one round of holidays. These impressions were very soon obliterated. I found it to be very earnest, and in many ways irksome. But whilst mornings were fine and winter not too near, toil had its compensations. From sallying out from home at half-past six I could have a good hour's reading on the road, and time went pleasantly on its way.

This kind of life I led for a period of nine years, continuing, with the exception of a short interval, my morning and evening walks, with the lark and thrush for my companions in summer, and my time beguiled in winter by not over agreeable splashes in mud and water, or in keeping my perpendicular when King Frost held sway. The footpath was in a wretched state during all those years, and lamps had not been introduced beyond the boundary of the borough at Miles Platting. But sometimes there was a merry gang of us, dropping off one by one, until I had to finish the journey alone. Practical joking was much indulged in; and we thought nothing of pushing each other into a deep ditch where now stands some of the best shop property in Newton Heath.

Monday mornings had their special attractions; and I have sometimes wished Sunday to be over that I might participate in the fun that for an hour or so would be rife in a corner of the room we worked in which we called "Paradise." Coming from all parts of the suburbs my shopmates had always something new to relate; and it is to these weekly gatherings that I attribute much of the bent of mind that has distinguished my after life.

It was during the first year of my connection with Manchester that I made the acquaintance of Elijah Ridings, the poet. He at that time kept a bookstall in Withy Grove. I frequently called in the dinner hour to look over his stock of books, until I got on chatting terms with him. Seeing that I was a country lad he began to ask me questions about my "come fro';" and I was only too delighted to give him all the information I could.

"Ay, an' art thou James Breerley lad," Elijah exclaimed, after I had given him "the story of my life from year to year." "Well, then thy mother would be Esther Whitehead?" I told him that was my mother's maiden name. "Ay, ay, I knew her. Hoo used to sing under my feyther at Newton Church. Ax her if hoo knew owd Jim Ridings. Here's a book o' mine I'll gie thee, an' I'll put my name in it."

This recognition so flattered me that I was encouraged to show the old poet a few lines I had written, but had not the temerity to offer them for publication. He read them over; and I could see that he was interested in that first attempt. "An' has thou written this?" he asked, when he had read the scrap. I owned, with not a little pride, that I was responsible for its production. "Here, I'll gie thee a note to John Bolton Rogerson. He's th' editor o' th' *Oddfellows' Magazine*; an' his office is i' Dale-street." I felt so proud of the introduction that I lost no time before calling upon Rogerson, who received me cordially, and promised my poem should appear in the next issue of the magazine. This promise he kept; and I had the pleasure of seeing my name for the first time in print.

My acquaintance with Rogerson led to my contributing several poems to the *Oddfellows' Magazine*. It led to other things also, some of which I cannot recall without a desire, as a Yankee would say, "to kick myself down stairs." An amateur performance was being got up at the Theatre Royal in aid of one of the Manchester charities; and I expressed a wish to Rogerson that I might be allowed to play a small part on that occasion.

"Have you been on the stage at all?" he asked of me. Had I not? I admitted with some hesitation, and I daresay a good deal of colour, that I had played "Iago," and "Virginius," besides several comic parts, chiefly Irish. He would lay the matter before the promoters of the performance, and acquaint me with their decision. The result was that they cast me in a very small part (John Burr) in the principal piece, John Bull; and a rehearsal was called. This was to take place at "Hayward's Hotel," where now stands the Queen's Theatre. I attended, but soon discovered that I had not the beardless enthusiasts of Pole Lane School for my stage companions. Principally they were the young "bloods" of the town I had to appear among; gentlemen with curly hair and kid gloves; the only person approaching years being my, now, friend William Doherty, then and still of Sugar Lane. Imagine me in the carpeted room of a grand hotel for the first time, my neck wrapped in a red worsted "comforter," and wearing a coat that might have been a cast-off of "Smike's," and the reader will not have much difficulty in guessing what my feelings were likely to be. Just before it came to my turn to rehearse, and without saying a word, I made a clean bolt out of the room, took three or four steps down stairs, and durst not breathe until I found myself in Deansgate, so dosed with anti-theatrical medicine that the disease returned not for a long time. Nineteen years after this occurrence I was playing in my own piece at the old Queen's Theatre ; and having bowed to my first call before the curtain I was met by a couple of gentlemen at the wing, with congratulations upon my success. There was no need of their introducing themselves to me. I recognised them at once as two of my old acquaintances of Hayward's Hotel memory. They are the only two left of that fine band of amateurs.

If cured for a time of my passion for the stage I was still haunted by visions of poetic greatness. But these came by fits and starts, and I am afraid were obscured by dissipations into which a new companionship led me. Years of the best time of life were being wasted in the sowing of wild oats and reaping the harvest. But one morning in the May of 1854 I was returning home after a late day's work at "stock-taking." Feeling tired and dirty, I stopped at a public-house trough at Miles Platting, and had a refreshing ablution. As I leaned against the trough whilst I wiped my face with my pocket-handkerchief I heard a lark singing overhead. I stood listening for some time, and that early song gave me an inspiration that I had not felt before. The idea of writing something on "May" rendered the rest of my journey a light one ; and as the breaking day was to be a holiday I determined upon writing something while the fit was on me. Reaching home I retired to bed, but not to sleep until the day was fully awake, when I dozed over. In my sleep my dreams were of Maytime; and the following lines were composed before I awoke—

"Whilst Dryads, decked in dewy gems,
   Gaily trip it o'er the lea,
To tiny bells, on nodding stems,
   Ringing elfin minstrelsy."

Whether anything more had been composed in sleep, and had faded from my dreaming memory, I can only have the faintest idea;

but the four lines are of a different measure to the rest of the poem. I completed my task that day, and sent the result to the *Manchester Guardian*, then published bi-weekly. It appeared in that paper, with an eulogium from the editor.

The autumn of that year deprived me of my mother, and I may say my home, as I never felt it to be home afterwards. The poor creature had been bedfast for months; and I was not acquainted with the cause of her death until after she was buried. It was cancer in the stomach; and her sufferings must have been intense. I shall never forget the day before she died. It was Saturday; and in the afternoon her only aunt, and bearing the same christian name, had called to see her. I was in the house at the time, when my father and I were startled by hearing from the room above a sound so strange, we thought, that we had to listen again. My dying mother and her aged aunt were singing " Glory to Thee; " the former's voice coming out as powerful as I had heard it in her earlier womanhood. On the Sunday evening I and my brother were called upstairs; and in a few minutes afterwards as good a woman as ever breathed the breath of life expired in my arms. Would to God there were more such women than there are!

Such was my attachment to the memory of my mother that I half resolved to remain a bachelor to the end of my days if I could not find a being like her, and bearing the same christian name. But there happened to be a girl working in a room over the warping-room in York-street that had attracted my attention. A country girl she was, fresh from the breezy uplands of Bowlee, with light wavy hair, and a face on which Honesty had put its stamp. One evening as we were leaving the warehouse I made up my mind to speak to her. " Thou'll get bagged ift' does," said a shopmate, as we walked up Oldham-road together, and behind this girl and her companions. " I'll risk being ' bagged '," I said. My uncle was very strict. I spoke to her the same evening; and during the conversation we had I elicited from her that her christian name was " Esther." That settled my bachelorhood. For twenty-nine years, come the 29th of the present month, that girl has been My Wife. I have not yet lived to deplore the circumstances under which we first met.

Shortly before we were married, my uncle (the manager) died. Whether it was through jealousy, being myself related to the firm, or from some other cause, I never knew, his successor, ere the " funeral baked meats " could have been consumed, bade me " make up my book." For the first time in my life I found myself " out of work." I remained in this state during ten weeks. The wedding day had been fixed ; and sooner than commit a " breach of promise," the girl I had set my heart upon took me " for better for worse." At that time I had not a penny to call my own. Fortune favoured me soon afterwards. I obtained employment in a silk warehouse, Brotherton and Green's, in Fountain Street ; and the first week— Whit-week of all others—I had to work until nine o'clock every night, and on the Saturday until ten ; but when I received my wages, considerably more than I had earned at any other time, and felt the joy that I had in store for my young wife, it was more of a holiday time for me than if I had been " cheap tripping " all the week.

It was whilst employed at this warehouse, and the out-come of a holiday caused by the rejoicings over the fall of Sebastopol, that I wrote my first sketch of any note—" A Day Out ; or a Summer Ramble in Daisy Nook." It was an extraordinary success. The story was first published in Abel Heywood's *Manchester Spectator* ; and afterwards reprinted by David Kelly, of Market Street. Of that work the *Manchester Guardian* said—

This amusing " Sketch of Lancashire life and character," just published by Mr Kelly, of Market Street (pp. 64), we learn is the production of Benjamin Brierley, an operative warper. Besides a vein of quiet humour, and a strong relish for the broad Doric dialect of the district, there is in this little book a fine manly tone, combined with a love of poetry and of nature, which give to its pages their strongest and subtlest charm. Many will be the inquiries of its readers for that sweet little spot " Daisy Nook," and even Saturday afternoon pedestrians will be exploring the country in various directions, casting wistful eyes, about th' edge o' dark, in search of " Red Bill's " village hostelry, with its toasted cheese and " milk o' Paradise." This little book is a welcome addition to our local literature, and doubly so as a revelation of " the warp and weft " that is amongst our workers.

The *Examiner and Times* followed with—

The intelligence of Lancashire men among the middle and working classes has often been made known to us both by speech and pen. Few counties, we believe, have given more frequent examples of what may be called an almost instinctive knowledge in the art of literary composition. It is a source of surprise, to all who take an interest in such characteristics, that men of so limited an amount of education, as many of our Lancashire writers, should still be able to give utterance to thought, feeling, or observation, in a manner so correct, and often as graphic. In the pages of Samuel Bamford, of Edwin Waugh, of John C. Prince, there is to be found, in numerous instances, an order of writing that would be envied by the most experienced. The little volume before us (" A Day Out.") presents a new aspirant for literary fame, and one who has undoubted facility and power. Mr. Brierley's humour is of the true racy character, as sterling in its way as Tim Bobbin or Cervantes. When he has fairly got into his theme, we have a laugh bubbling over in every line. Nor is there less cleverness in the gift he possesses of scene painting. Like the rest of his compeers, he goes out into the woods or over the moors and feels their refreshing influences. He writes of what he sees and what he feels; there is no second-hand love of the beautiful about him. The man who can give us such pictures has more in store, and we trust he will not hide his talents under a bushel.

Afterwards came the *Oldham Advertiser* with—

" A Day Out " is unquestionably one of those little gems of local literature which it is not often our good fortune to meet with. It is precisely what its title indicates it to be—a day's ramble; but a ramble in which incidents, some the most affecting, and others the most humorous, crowd one upon another, never permitting the interest to flag, from the departure amid the " confusion of clogs that prevailed all over the teeming streets of the great commercial Babel, Manchester," to the return, welcomed by " the brightest of sunshine, a woman's look of love."

" A Day Out " is a thoroughly Lancashire book. The scenery through which the reader is invited to ramble is Lancashire; the habits he is requested to observe are Lancashire; the characters to whom he is introduced are Lancashire, many of whom in the rich and racy Lancashire dialect express sentiments worthy of kings, and sense that would not disgrace philosophers. This being the case, it cannot but become a favourite with Lancashire readers; and as they peruse it the manly pathos of " Hobson " will not fail to garnish with pearl drops their optics, whilst the quaint shrewdness and quietly flowing humour of " Owd Israel " will most certainly excite their risibility, until it will break its reins and rush off in a runaway gallop.

The *Athenæum*, however, cut me up fearfully; and in my second venture even worse. But the *Saturday Review*, on the contrary, could afford to give me three columns of a splendid notice.

Work being slack at Messrs. Brotherton and Green's I obtained a similar situation at Messrs. Brennan and Sons, Church Street. Here I remained several years, during which time I wrote " Bunk Ho," and some of the shorter sketches included in my second volume, published under the title of " Chronicles of Waverlow." I was now, as a labourer would say, " fairly on the job." I left this situation—not before it was time to leave it, things being so bad— to fulfil a sub-editorship on the *Oldham Times*. For that season-able change I have to thank my friend Charles Potter, then a struggling, but now eminent artist. After a year of scissors-and-paste work I removed to London, thinking to make my mark there. I missed it, however; but my experience in the " great metrolipus " was something to feel proud of for a lifetime. I was a frequent visitor at the Savage Club; and was hand and glove with all the Broughs, Andrew Haliday, T. W. Robertson, Leicester Bucking-

ham, Dr. Strauss, and "Little Prowse" of the *Daily Telegraph.*
The work finished that I had gone to do I returned to Manchester,
and completed a story I had commenced in London, "The Layrock
of Langleyside," the first serial published in the *Manchester Weekly
Times.*

Such flattering notices did I receive from the press and the
public that I was induced to continue my work, and adopt
literature as my profession. I was entering upon a perilous path,
and one that would have made me pause at the very gate could I
have foreseen the dangers and vicissitudes I would have to
encounter. But notwithstanding the cloud that the *Athenæum*
had cast over it there was a tempting brightness beyond. I was,
however, sometimes disheartened when I reflected on the number
of well educated people, with wealth and influence at their back,
who had failed to reach Parnassus; and I, a poor hand-loom
weaver, was attempting that which had been impossible with them.
But at these desponding times there would come a seasonable note
of encouragement that buoyed me up, and gave me a new impulse.
The *Athenæum*, after chastening me, took me kindly in its arms,
and said good things of my "Layrock of Langleyside." There
came from another source, and one that I could not have
anticipated, a lengthy review of which the following is an
extract. Speaking of me and my works generally, the writer
says :—

A self taught man, he possesses in a wonderful degree the power of
describing, in plain, good old Saxon language, the scenes around him, and
of painting, with all the power and vigour of another Hogarth, the
worthy, true-hearted, open-handed, brave Lancashire men and women.
Humour, quaint and old-world like, yet genial as the newest day in summer—at times subdued and calm as the smile on the face of a sleeping
child, or gushing forth joyously—yet ever humour; pathos, touching and
tender as the face of your dear dead girl, and leaving a sadness in your
heart, and the tears in your eyes; and wit, bright and cutting as a
Damascus blade, and bending like one, are thrown together in the same
pages with a magical power; and the smile, the hearty laugh, and the
quiet tear, are created by reading almost any one of Mr. Brierley's stories.
The creation of such real, lasting feelings is the most blessed privilege
of true genius; it is true art, not art acquired by studying cold, dry rules,
but the art in-born, and therefore God-given, and part of the soul. It may
seem a simple thing to make the human heart thrill with joy, or throb
with pain, but in the sense we speak of, genius, and genius alone can play
upon the wondrous harp, evoking wild, sad laments, or glorious gushes of
thankful praise. Benjamin Brierley can do this, and the laughter he
creates is as healthy as the tears you cannot keep back when he introduces
you to such men as "Hobson" and "Shadow." We may laugh at many
of the couplets of Byron's Don Juan, or at the witty things in Sterne,

hiding as they do some *double entendre*, and be ever so much the worse for such laughter; but between Mr. Brierley's pure mirth—real mirth, smelling, so to speak, of the May blossom and the newly-turned earth, there is a great gulf fixed, and as much difference as there is between the hollow, graveyard laugh of a poor consumptive *fille de publique*, and the sweet ringing notes of a pure loving maiden.

Perhaps it may be thought that a reviewer has nothing whatever to do with an author's every-day life, and doubtless people wisely refrain from prying too closely into the private life of those whose lot it is to amuse and improve them. To a certain extent this want of curiosity is commendable, but when an author's life shines through his writings, curiosity is very pardonable. Byron's life shone through his army of Laras, Giaours, and Corsairs! Wordsworth's shone through his quiet, holy philosophy; and Keats's life with its vast yearnings after the divine spirit of beauty, shone through his Endymion. Mr. Brierley's life shines out in his volumes, in one or two wild, passionate prayers for the weal of his toiling brothers, in that (doubtless autobiographical) story of "Dragged Up," and in that manly, sensible dedication of one of his books to "the gentlemen who found the author in obscurity, and helped to drag him out of it." Born to a life of toil, with fears of a life of vagabondage darkening over him—thrown in the very heart of circumstances calculated to grind out the very soul, and to make man into a mere machine—Benjamin Brierley has gone on his way manfully, with the courage of a true hero, facing life in its darkest phases, and conquering one by one all the unfavourable things, and converting them to his own use, until at length he stands in a worthy, well-earned position, won by the force of his stern determination, and the wise and good use of his faculties—a notable example to others of his own class, bidding them with clarion note persevere in the right path; and also a bright and shining proof to those of the classes higher in social position, that God's gift are catholic, and are bestowed upon many whose only misfortune is that they have not the opportunities enjoyed or neglected by those who consider themselves of a different and superior order. A proof or a lesson like this is worth ever so many sermons, for it tells of real life, real conquest, real heroism, upon which we may, in all humility, believe the Master "who went about doing good," looks with pleasure.

Who could have faltered by the way after such a kindly lift. The notice appeared in the *Preston Chronicle*, and the writer has since been a contributor to the pages of the journal that bears my name.

Following my first effort at serial writing came my story of "Irkdale," which was also contributed to the *Manchester Weekly Times*. I had written two lengthy sketches for the *Oldham Times*, "Treadlepin Fold," and "The New Borough," but I could hardly call them stories. "Irkdale" was a more ambitious work, and when completed in the *Weekly Times* was re-issued in two volumes by Messrs. Tinsley Brothers, London. While writing this story I and my wife, with a little girl, the only offspring I have been blessed with, temporarily left our home in Manchester to rusticate in the Unitarian parsonage at Stand, in Pilkington; my reverend friend the pastor, with his family, going on the continent to spend the summer and autumn in travel. In this secluded mansion I spent some of the happiest days of my married life. For neighbours I had the late Mr. Archibald Winterbottom—all honour to his memory!—and Richard Rome Bealey, author of "After Business Jottings," and other poems. I was a country gentleman for a time, walking out with my dog on an evening, and chatting with old people by the way. This dog was called "Fly," and was a remarkable animal. She could distinguish the sound of the door bell from that of any other; and whenever I had occasion to go to the post office, nearly a mile distant, she would paw at my door when I was ready to start, to accompany me. I have often wondered how she knew the time. After posting my letters I sometimes crossed over to the "Church Inn," where on an evening a "gradely sort" of company met, and whose friendship in after life became, as it were, a part of my being. "Fly" had learnt the way to this jovial hostelry, and would hide herself under the seat until I was ready to go home.

I was on a visit to my old friend the parson after his return home; and during the conversation I had with him he seemed to remember something that caused him to indulge in a quiet chuckle. "Mister Brierley," he said at last, "I think you taught 'Fly' bad manners while you were here." "Why did he think so?" I asked. "Well," he replied, good humouredly, "I went the other day to the post-office, and when I had posted my letters 'Fly' trotted over to the 'Church Inn.' I think she must have been there before." I owned to the "soft impeachment."

On leaving Stand I was anxious to do something that would keep my memory fresh among my new friends, and as a memento of the many happy days I had spent in the neighbourhood of Whitefield. I named the matter to one of these *sinners* who frequented the Church Inn, and he thought that if I got up an entertainment at the Church School, the proceeds of which should be devoted to the providing a dinner for the resident old people, it would be as good a thing as any that could be done. I fell in with his views, and the project was warmly taken up by his brother sinners. A committee was organized at once, and action commenced. The proceeds of the entertainment were to be supplemented by subscriptions in order to raise a good fund. A well-known gentleman, wealthy, but with "ways of his own," was asked to subscribe. No, not a farthing would he give; but he would take a front seat ticket for the concert, and pay for it whether he attended or not. For this he handed as payment—not three shillings—but £25.

The entertainment and the subscriptions were highly successful, so much so that on a certain day, I cannot now remember the date, 550 people of both sexes over the age of sixty, and resident in the township of Pilkington, were entertained at dinner in the Stand Church School. The event was notified by a general holiday throughout the district. Those of the old people who were too infirm to walk were conveyed to the school, and home again, in 'busses and cabs; and it was an interesting sight to see many who had never ridden in either before swaying helplessly to and fro' as they jogged on their way. On their departure the remainder of the fund was distributed in money—to those over sixty and under seventy, a shilling each; to those over seventy and under eighty, eighteenpence; and to those over eighty, two shillings. Seeing this result of a few words dropped in a friendly ear, it was not a matter of regret to me that for a few months I had made my home in the neighbourhood of Whitefield.

I again settled near Queen's Park in Collyhurst. Here I wrote my third serial story, " My Grandmother's Clockcase," which is the only one—I know not why—that has not appeared in book form. Here " Ab-o'th'-Yate " makes his first appearance as a prominent character; and he has been playing his eccentricities on the public, in various ways and moods, ever since. This story was followed by " Red Windows Hall," which, with the exception of a small dramatic sketch, entitled " The Fratchingtons of Fratchingthorpe," was my last original contribution to the columns of the *Manchester Weekly Times*. But our acquaintance has been renewed in another form.

At this time Mr. Charles Potter, the now successful artist, was struggling with his profession, as all men have to struggle whose social position is on a low level. As a weaver in a factory he had done some remarkable work, and it was predicted of him that he would sometime grasp a very elevated rung on the ladder of fame, a forecast which has been realised. The three of us were frequently in each other's society, and if Benny, or Jimmy, or Charlie could have " brewed a peck o' maut," they might have been as jolly as the happy trio that Burns has immortalised. There were others about us starting to make a mark in life, and have made it, but in other professions than literature and art. The Dumvilles sprang from Hollinwood, and have been eminent in music.

I remember becoming acquainted, when I was younger, with a very strange man, as I took him to be, who sometimes visited my father. They were cronies in politics, and at times their conversation was quite interesting to me. Samuel Collins, or " Owd Sam," as he was mostly called, was a genius in a way. He never spoke at random, like some politicians who are determined to say something, whether it is worth listening to or not; but seemed to weigh his words, and speak with a hesitancy that led one to think he did not feel sure that his opinion was the correct one. At these times he would cast his eyes up at the ceiling, and deliver himself with a chuckle, as if to say " take it for what it is worth, if it is worth anything." I knew that he had been *accused* of writing poetry, which was quite as offensive in a working man as wearing polished shoes on a weekday; but I had not seen any of it. Somehow it came about that a number of gentlemen, among whom were my friends Dronsfield and Potter, began to interest themselves on " Owd Sam's " account; and the result was a subscription list being opened to enable Collins to publish an edition of his poems. I took up the task of editing the little volume, and of writing a biographical sketch as an introduction. The following are extracts from it—

" The author of this unassuming little volume was born on the 1st December, 1802. His parents were then living in an old-fashioned cottage in Drury Lane, near the turnpike road leading from Manchester to Oldham. Samuel was the youngest of a numerous family, seven of whom have lived to be fathers and mothers. Only two survive (1859)—the worthy subject of this notice and a sister. * * * It can readily be imagined from subsequent characteristics that Samuel Collins was one of those beings whom our grandmothers were apt to distinguish by the term " old-fashioned children," as he no sooner got out of his " dadins " than manifestations of an artistic bent began to show themselves. Drawing chalk figures on the house flags, cutting models in paper, were his first essays in a pursuit which, whatever might have been his early attachment, seems to have been abandoned in after years. It was not, however, until he had obtained those objects dear to aspiring children—a box of paints, and a veritable camel's hair pencil—that art found itself deserted by our youthful votary, as, from what I can learn, it appears that through his manner of handling the pencil, during the production of farm-yards, hare and hounds, race horses, &c., he acquired a habit that seriously interfered with his progress in the art of penmanship. Oftentimes might he be seen squatting by the side of his mother, who instructed him in her

62

homely manner whilst she plied the bobbinwheel. How much of poetry may have been drunk in at this period ?

* * * * * * *

" Like a good many of his brethren, who have been condemned to hopeless ignorance through the misfortune of being poor, Collins when very young was put to work. He became bobbin-winder to those in advance of him. The younger branches of a weaver's family know how to appreciate such an infliction, for their portion of the ordeal is the most trying; and it is no wonder that they should take to wooden creations of ' Punch and Judy,' bird-nesting, and even donkey-riding (who has not indulged in the latter ?), rather than be tied to the three-legged stool, and be heart-sickened by the never-ending supply of ' empties.' The bent of Collins' moral disposition was not, however, that of his doubtlessly vivacious companions. He was given to seek retirement and meditation. Such is the natural bias of a mind instinctively imbued with poetic feelings. When other boys were at play he was, perhaps, poring over the pages of some historical work, for he was partially fond of history, especially that of his native land. * * *

" When about thirteen years of age Collins confesses to have *perpetrated* his first song, which was on the occasion of a game at ' I spy.' He was sent out along with others to hide, and one of his companions, ' Nut Bradley,' slipped the rest, and crept into a cart in which a number of girls were playing. The song was to record the fact. One verse read as follows :—

> " One neet as we wur playin' at ' I spy,'
> There wur Nut Bradley, John Bocky, and I,
> We went to hoide us, Nut fro' us did part,
> An' went among th' wenches i' owd George's cart."

Collins' peculiar humour is shown in the following couplet, taken from his " Rural Walk ":—

> " I'm almost lost in reverie, till some
> Stray *cuckoo* shouts, and then I think of *home*."

A couple of stanzas from the same poem will close this notice. They are quite characteristic.

> " A vivid flash, a distant rumbling noise,
> A few large drops come pattering as I pass ;
> A holly bush a shelter now supplies,
> And snug, and safe, and quite secure I was.

An object comes, so dazzling to men's eyes—
    Another flash ? No, no! a lovely lass
Comes tripping by, I askéd her to stay
    And shelter take, she smiled, and tripped away.

" And that said smile illumined half the sky,
    And shed a halo 'mid the dark'ning gloom ;
Her faultless form I followed with my eye,
    And wondered what would be the early doom
Of that fair nymph ? Could man or time destroy
    Such blushing innocence, such rosy bloom ?
A monitor within me cried—' Old sinner,
    Think of th' old dame who's cooking thee thy dinner.'"

My acquaintance with James Dronsfield led to my being brought
into contact with the author of " Passages in the life of a Radical."
I had met him once before, but it was in company with a number
of others, and at a time when authorship had never entered into
my dreams. He was living at that time in Charlestown, Blackley,
at a cottage he thus alludes to in one of his poems :—

" I think of my cottage full many a time,
    A nest among flowers at midsummer prime ;
    With sweet pink, and white rock, and bonny rose bower,
And honeybine garland o'er window and door ;
As prim as a bride e'er the revels begin,
And as white as a lily without and within."

It was while serving an aprenticeship in Blackley that Mr.
Dronsfield became acquainted with old Sam, who was then getting
just beyond the prime of life. He had often seen the poet striding
sturdily along Valentine Brow, and at length he ventured to speak
to him. That casual acquaintance ripened into a friendship that
lasted until the elder of the two was laid in Middleton Churchyard.

My intimate acquaintance with Bamford did not begin until his
return to Lancashire from what he chose to call his " exile " in
London. He took a small cottage in Hall Street, Moston, and commenced life anew at over seventy, on a capital of twelve shillings,
with a wife whom the shocks of fortune had nearly shaken to pieces.

As a means of obtaining a livelihood old Sam commenced giving
readings in public, not confined to his own works, but embracing
some of Tennyson's. In this pursuit he was never very successful.
His antiquated style of delivery often provoked merriment when it
was not intended ; and a peculiar stammer which he could not

overcome was another source of fun. I assisted him on several occasions, one of which stands prominently in my recollection. We were at the Salford Town Hall, and there was a fair audience. Sam had got a new copy of his "Passagess" from which to read; and he had omitted to cut a portion of it that was among his selections. On coming to this part of the book he could not connect the matter so as to make sense of it. He turned the leaves backwards and forwards, "hummed," and "ayed"—but still he could not discover the connection. The audience tittered; the reader perspired; when at length it occurred to him that the leaves had not been cut. He felt for his knife, which was missing from his pocket. In his exasperation, and when the audience were getting noisy, he inserted his fingers betwixt the leaves, and ripped them open, accompanying the act with a little mild profanity which was not in the programme.

I remember his calling upon me one morning when I was busy with the introduction to my "Chronicles of Waverlow." He saw a portrait of mine that had been painted by a local artist. His criticism was not very flattering. "Wheay, lad," he said, after gazing at it for a few minutes, "theau favvors a carter donned up'." I submitted to him a passage in the article I was writing in which his name appeared, and told him that I intended asking him if I might publish it. "Read it," he said. I read as follows:—

"I have seen honest old Samuel Bamford sweat as if suffering from some acute pain on reading a stranger's account of Lancashire people." "May I use it in that form?" I asked. "Ay," he replied, " an', an', an' put an honest d—n or two in it."

Bamford's great misfortune, the loss of his only child in her early womanhood, always impressed me with a painful feeling, because I had a presentiment that such would be my lot. I had my only one—bearing the same Christian name. We had both been hand-loom weavers, and shared poverty alike. The affinity of every circumstance appalled me whenever the idea crossed my mind, and that was often, until it became the one thought of my life. The blow came at last. In her nineteenth year ours was taken from us, and the desolate feeling of my old friend had become mine. But of that in its place. Still I cannot but exclaim with Bamford—

" The dearest gem
That e'er was treasured near a parent's heart;
Too pure a gem
For human life, to Heaven she must depart!

Oh ! child of love,
Let us behold thee, earthward if thou stray !
Come from above
On radiant wing, come in thy bright array !

" Oh ! blessed one,
Could we behold thee even as thou wert,
Call thee our own
And press our angel unto mortal heart !
Then would these tears
Which oft have flowed since thy dying hour,
Dark months and years,
Be stayed—thou still would'st have that soothing power."

Bamford had arranged with Alexander Ireland and Co. for a re-print of his poems ; but the old man's sight had failed him, and he could not undertake the work of revising and editing. I was then living at Whitefield, and as my time was not fully occupied I undertook to do the work for him, going to his house in Moston once a week for the purpose. I had a tough job with him. He would adhere to quaint forms of spelling that jarred on my ear. I had many a tiff with him, but he always worsted me by asserting his right to do what he liked with his own property. He would often get into a passion, and did not care what he said at such times. For example, there was his poem addressed to " My Wynder." Why spell it with a *y* when it was unnecessary, as *i* gave the same sound both in the dialect and in proper English ? " It does be d——d as like !" he exclaimed with plenty of warmth ; " w-i-n-d-e-r would be *winder*," he said, sounding the *i* as in *window*. "An' if theau spells it that way I'll bag thee." It was no use contending further ; I had to give way.

Being invited to a " Literary Dinner " by the then Mayor of Manchester (Mr. John Grave), I was appointed to wait upon Old Sam with the Mayor's carriage, and bring him to Mount House, Cheetham, " wilta-shalta." I had much difficulty in executing my commission, meeting with rebuffs of no very pleasant character. *He* was not going to be taken like a " madman " with a " keeper." He knew his way, and could walk it. We agreed at last to reverse matters, he must take me ; so with that understanding I got him into the carriage, and drove to Mount House. When the dinner was over the carriage was again at our service. I had it in my mind to take Bamford home, and call at my own house on my way back. But Sam had arranged otherwise. Without acquainting me with his intentions he landed me at my own door, which was attended to by my wife. "Here, missis," he said, "I've browt this lad o' yor's whoam." Then with a chuckle he drove off.

When left alone in the world Bamford seemed to take a pleasure in visiting the grave of his wife and daughter in Middleton Church-yard. I accompanied him on one of these visits, and read on the stone the inscription on the grave of not only the dead but the living. At the foot of the inscription recording his wife's death I found the following, which had been inscribed in anticipation,— " Also Samuel Bamford, who died ———— , aged ——." What a strange idea, I thought. But it was not long ere the blanks were filled up.

The last time I saw him outside his house was on a warm summer day, sitting with his back against a wall opposite his door. He was so near being blind that he could only recognise me by my voice. He had a group of children around him to whom he was distributing toffies. He was fond of sweets himself, and often carried them in his pocket. Now the children would sing a verse of a hymn which he would lead out two lines at a time, after the old Wesleyan fashion ; then he would lean back, and with his eyes raised to heaven, listen devoutly to the singing. Who knows what voices he heard in that singing, or in whose presence he felt ? Did he feel " the touch of a vanished hand," or did he hear " the sound of a voice that *was* still ?" I stood some time looking on the scene before I made my presence known to the old man, as I did not wish to disturb what appeared to me to be a foretaste of something not far removed from those tremulous lips that were joining in that childish service. The next time I saw him he had taken his bed, from which he was eager to be removed. A smile dwelt upon his face as he gave utterance to these words, the last he spoke in my hearing, and which deeply impressed me, " I'm gettin' close to th' edge of eternity ; I shall rowl o'er soon." He did " rowl o'er " in a few days after ; and thus ended the life of a man who had led an almost blameless life, and had known his share of human suffering.

My " Daisy Nook Sketches " gave me the *entree* to a social and literary circle, who occasionally foregathered in the coffee room of the Clarence Hotel. There was a geniality in the spirit that presided over these meetings which seems to have departed with the building, and not been found anywhere else. It has not joined any club, or social gathering of any name. Perhaps it has been "blackballed." From the centre of the table the tree sprang which is now and has since been known as the *Manchester Literary Club.* Of the planters of that tree, only five are living :—Edwin Waugh, Charles Hardwick, John Page, R. R. Bealey, and myself. Our first location was the Cathedral Hotel, then kept by Mr. D. T. Batty, the well-known numismatist, now of the Cathedral Yard. Since that time, the club has moved about from place to place, like a spirit that could find no rest. Of the earlier members, seventeen were photographed in a group by Mr Bentley of Buxton. Of the seventeen, eleven have gone home, amongst the number being Charles Swain, John Harland, Sam Bamford, T. T. Wilkinson, of Burnley, David Morris, and J. P. Stokes, who formed the central figures of the group. Another of the departed, Joseph Chattwood, the then president, sat at one of the wings. I remember when, some years ago, Mr. T. T. Wilkinson and I were looking at the picture, Mr. Wilkinson remarking : " That group has lost its front teeth." It was not many weeks before his own death made another gap. The club has celebrated its " coming of age," and can now afford to snap its fingers at its parents, if so disposed ; but no doubt it remembers with a kindly thought the men to whom it owes its existence.

I had been introduced to Mr. Waugh previous to these gatherings at the Clarence Hotel. When he published his celebrated poem, " Come whoam to the childer an' me," his name was in everybody's mouth ; and at a Soiree held at the house of Mr. John Bolton Rogerson, he was one of the guests. I, as one of the promoters of the gathering, was brought in contact with this " Moorland Minstrel," and a friendship grew out of that meeting. Many a tussle have we had with fortune since that time, some of which we have shared together. I remember our joining in an entertainment at Blackpool during the " season." The place was crowded at the time—I do not mean the room in which the entertainment was given, but the town. We had three nights of it ; but the weather was against us. If it was wet people would not turn out ; if it was fine they would not turn in, so the whole thing was a " frost "—it did not even clear expenses. On the third evening, when we were " squaring up," as far as we could, a little dog put its paws on Waugh's knee, and wagged its tail as if delighted at making his acquaintance. " Ah, lad," said Waugh, patting the dog's neck, " *theau* hasno' bin givin' entertainments."

On another occasion—I might as well say, it was my daughter's eleventh birthday—my wife made a party, and invited eleven of my daughter's schoolmates to take part in the proceedings. There was one person invited who was not a schoolmate, and that was Edwin Waugh. Things went on gaily with the youngsters; and whilst I was assisting my wife in preparing supper, I heard a loud yell of delight proceeding from the parlour. Eager to ascertain what was the cause of all this fun, I entered the room. There was a sight for a student in natural history—Waugh on all-fours, pacing round the room with two children on his back, "doing the Belle Vue Elephant," and now and then giving a roar, after the manner of the well-known *pachyderm* who carries all sizes and ages of children round the "course" at the zoological gardens in Hyde Road.

I owe something to Edwin. It was he who introduced me to the *Manchester Weekly Times*, then edited by Mr. Henry Barry Peacock. In the supplement of that journal, most of my earlier work has appeared.

Some years before these incidents occurred I had not met with Edwin Waugh for a long time. This apparent estrangement induced me to pen the following lines :—

TO EDWIN WAUGH.

"What ails thee," Ned? Theaw'rt not as 'twur,
Or else no' what aw took thee for,
When fust theaw made sich noyse an' stir
   I' this quare pleck.
Hast' flown at Fame wi' sich a ber,
   As t' break thi neck?

Or arta droppin' fithers, eh;
An' keepin' th' neest warm till some day,
Toart April-tide, or sunny May,
   When theaw may'st spring,
An' warble eaut a new-made lay,
   On strengthened wing?

For brids o' sung mun ha' ther meawt,
As weel as other brids, aw deawt;
But though they peearch beneath a speaut,
   Or roost 'mung heather,
They're saved fro' mony a shiverin' beaut,
   By hutchin' t'gether.

69

Come, let Owd Moather Dumps a-be,
An' wag thy yed wi' friendly glee;
Fly o'er, a humble brid to see.
　　　　　This world is wide;
Ther's reawm for booath thee an' me,
　　　　　An' moore beside.

Come, scrat' thy bill, an' bat thy wings;
Hark heaw the merry "Layrock" sings!
Good news fro' fleawerlond he brings
　　　　　In his glad throat;
An' conno' theaw, 'mung lesser things,
　　　　　Put in a note?

The buds that peep fro' every spray;
The cock that wakkens up the day;
The thrush that sings its reaundelay
　　　　　I' beawer an' tree,
Sheaut—"Come, owd brid, an' have a say
　　　　　I' nature's spree!"

For 'tis a spree, this life o' eaurs;
Drinkin' wine fro' cups o' fleawers,
An' takkin' incense in i' sheawers,
　　　　　Enoogh to crack us;
Or havin' glorious neetly keawers
　　　　　Wi' a fithered Bacchus.

Fly o'er thisel, or if theaw chooses
To bring some other brids o'th' Muses,
Pike eaut a flock, an' come an' rooze this,
　　　　　My peearchin cote;
The meawt seize him who then refuses
　　　　　To tune his throat.

Foremost in flight, on gentle wing,
The "Prestwich Philomela"[1] bring.
It swells my crop to yer him sing,
　　　　　In plaintive strain;
To squeeze his claw wi' friendly wring
　　　　　Aw would be fain.

[1] Charles Swain; author of "The Mind," and other poems.

Then there's that owd gray-toppined lark,
Who sang when theaw an aw wur dark,
Lung yers sin', o'er toart th' " Little Park,"
   " Bamford "[2] his name ;
Let's give eaur yeds a reverent jark,
   An' own his fame.

Bring in thy train those brids o' note,
Blithe " Charlie,"[3] with his wattled throat ;
An' " Dick,"[4] who never sang nor wrote
   To hurt his fellow ;
With him,[5] who aye wi' " seed box " sote
   To mak' brids mellow.

Bring him who to the past still clings,[6]
Who in some moss-grown ruin sings,
Whilst delving down for bygone things
   I' tombs an' ditches ;
Neaw croonin' o'er the deeds o' kings,
   Or pranks o' witches.

An' bring that honest soul thy skoo in,[7]
Who *notes* what other brids are dooin' ;
Who at a " weed " is aulus pooin,
   To sweel his throttle ;
Who if he's mute is surely brewin'
   Some genial prattle.

An' bring that grizzly weazent wren,[8]
Who twitters nobbut neaw an' then ;
Who " ale " prescribes to " physic " men,
   An' brids as weel.
(If souls obeyed his guidin' ken,
   They'd starve the de'il.)

[2] Samuel Bamford ; author of " Passages in the Life of a Radical," etc., etc,
[3] Charles Hardwick ; author of the " History of Preston," etc.
[4] R. R. Bealey ; author of " After Business Jottings," etc.
[5] Joseph Chatwood ; president of the Manchester Literary Club.
[6] John Harland ; editor of " Baines' History of Lancashire."
[7] J. P. Stokes ; correspondent of the *Times*.
[8] Elijah Ridings ; author of the " Village Muse," etc.

An' to mak' up the festive cage,
Bring that plump brid, the " Happy Page ; " [9]
Who'd give in song the exact gauge
        Of throat o' viper, [10]
An' tell, by keawntin' fithers, th' age
        O' woodland piper.

Wi' hop an' twitter, chirp an' sung,
We'd drive the scamperin' heaurs alung ;
An' if thy glee, an 'Lijah's lung,
        I' tone should slacken,
Ther'd be enoogh o' Charlie's tongue
        To keep us wakken.

We'd ha' " Tim's Grave," an' "Th' Sweetheart Gate,"
An' " Owd Pegge's " cure for th' wakkerin' state ; [11]
An' " Jerry," [12] too, should shake his pate
        Wi' monkey claiver ;
An' if yo'rn short o' rhymin' prate,
        Aw'd croon " Th' Owd Wayver."

We met o' love an' friendship sing ;
O' Charity's exhaustless spring ;
O' Beauty, that wi' radiant wing,
        Charms brid and bard ;
An' then, for th' sake o'th' fun 'twould bring,
        Try th' jokin' " card." [13]

A neet o' sich like mirthfu' croozin',
No friend forgettin'—no foe abusin' ;
Neaw leaud i' sung, neaw sweetly musin',
        Were " bliss divine ;"
An' to the soul a deep infusin'
        O' Jove's best wine.

---

[*] John Page (Felix Folio) ; author of " Street Dealers and Quacks," etc.
[10] Mr. Page, in " Letters on Natural History," maintains that the viper, in time of danger, swallows its young.
[11] *Vide* " Ale *versus* Physic," by Elijah Ridings.
[12] Alluding to a humorous story about a " monkey," told with considerable gusto by Charles Hardwick.
[13] A term much used in conversation by one of the worthies above named.

Thus may we flutter through life's grove,
Neaw crackt wi' glee, neaw steeped i' love,
Till wingin' to that roost above,
   Where dwell the blest,
We find, like Noah's herald dove,
   A place o' rest.

It was during my temporary sojourn at Whitefield that my first acquaintance with John Critchley Prince was renewed. It was in a form that took me by surprise. A number of the frequenters of the "Albion," in Hough Lane, Lower Broughton, men well-to-do, were admirers of Prince's writings. These gentlemen, being informed of the poet's necessitous condition, resolved to get up a public dinner in his honour, and to present him with a purse of money. I was invited to take the chair, and felt proud of the position. Knowing Prince's weakness, and that he had not the power to say "No" if anyone asked him to have a glass of whisky, I took him severely under my care. He sat on my left during dinner, and when the table was cleared, I said to him, "Now, Prince, you are only to drink when I ask you." To this he did not offer a murmur. He was rather reticent than otherwise, but seemed to enjoy his associations. I was asked to recite one of his poems, a favourite of mine, an "Epistle to a Brother Poet." When I had finished, Prince turned to me, and said : "Ben, who wrote that ?" "You," I replied. He was quite overcome, and had to bury his face in his hands. He seemed to be a literary "Rip Van Winkle," trying to remember a former life.

He did not long survive that night. We had the melancholy task one day of bearing him to his last resting place in Hyde churchyard, the procession being headed by Edwin Waugh, John Page, and myself, and followed by a host of his literary confreres. What shocked most of us was the absence of the public in the streets. At an ordinary funeral, there is generally a lot of people congregated to see it ; but here, when a great poet, one of the "sweetest singers" that Lancashire ever gave birth to, is being borne to his rest, scarcely an eye is there to witness the proceedings. *Sic itur ad astra !*

One can hardly speak of Waugh without associating with his name that of Charles Hardwick. They are brothers in more senses than one, for they seem to have grown on the same tree. Ever genial Charlie ! When thy chin ceases to wag the world will seem to have lost one of its motors. But there is talk and talk.

Some people will weary you with incessantly "reeling off" nothing in their conversation. But although Hardwick will talk "an hour by the clock" there is sure to be common sense in every sentence, and instruction at the end of all. I remember an excursion party a number of us once had in the Lake district; there were about twenty of us, amongst the lot the president of the Literary Club. We were staying one night at the George Hotel, Bowness, and I was elected to occupy the same room as Mr. Hardwick. We all retired at the same time, but some of us were bound to be the last—Hardwick and I. The rest were at the end of the corridor when we were selecting our candles. "Just watch yond' two teawsels," said Chattwood, "I'll bet Brierley picks the shortest candle there is." As it happened, I did; but a shout of laughter followed that I could not understand the cause of; I found it out afterwards. Hardwick had selected the longest candle, and it was predicted by the company that there would be "summat like a dog battle before long," but they were deceived that night.

I was once in company with a prominent member of the Oldham District of the M.U. Oddfellows. During our conversation this gentlemen asked me if I knew Mr. Charles Hardwick, Editor of the Oddfellows' Magazine. I said I did. "Very fine fellow,' the gentleman remarked. I agreed with him. "He con mak' a speech off nowt, and say summat, too." "I beg your pardon," I said, "he is the most reticent man I know; I can hardly get a word out of him." The man looked at me earnestly for a moment, then, jerking himself round in his seat, said "yo' known nowt abeaut him, dun yo' be d————d." Honest old Charlie. He has done something more than talk in his time. His History of Preston is looked upon as a great authority, and no less so his books on the antiquities of Lancashire.

My acquaintance with Samuel Laycock began later in life. I had read, and admired some of his "pomes" years before I saw the man. I think I first met him at a concert given for his benefit at the Mechanics' Institution, Stalybridge. He was leaving that town to take a situation at Fleetwood, and the concert was meant as a farewell. I was never more deceived in the personal appearance of a man in my life. I had pictured him in my mind as being a robust, rollicking fellow. Instead of that I found him to be nearly all head, his body only attached to it as a kind of support. "Ab-o'th'-Yate" once said it was made of wire taken out of an "owd humbrell." My closer acquaintance with Sam was grown at Blackpool, where, after leaving Fleetwood, he commenced photographing. Whenever I went to that popular watering place I had to " sit," which occupation led to many a pleasant chat, and not a little banter. I remember him on one occasion getting his temper into a white heat as I sat waiting for the camera to fire at me. Sam was rubbing a glass with wash-leather at the time, and the harder he rubbed the friction on his mind seemed to keep company. Some one had been pirating one of his poems, " Bowton's Yard," I think it was, and he was going to put the pirate in court, which eventually he did, and obtained five pounds damages. " Sam, how is it ? nobody offers to steal anything of mine," I said. " Your name's not Laycock," was the reply. " Oh, I see." Meeting him at an entertainment at Blackpool in the October following, he asked me did I get many engagements to give readings ? " As many as I care to fulfil," I replied. " Strange! I get none," he remarked. " Your name's not Brierley," I said. Sam saw the point at once, and his face opened out into a grotesque grin, the prelude to a hearty laugh.

Moving in a sphere of poesy more Tennysonian than that which distinguished his Lancashire contemporaries, Charles Swain might have been termed the laureate of the north. The stream of his verse flows sweetly, and is never marred by the cropping up of those literary boulders which indicate that shallows are near.

" Though deep, yet clear, though gentle, yet not dull—
Strong without rage, without o'erflowing, full."

I was not personally acquainted with him in his mid-day life, but in his later years he seemed to me to live in the society of the ethereal. There was nothing savouring of worldliness in his character, or that would indicate an acquaintance with the exigencies and turmoil of " business." He was all soul. No one who had ever been in his presence would ever doubt his being a poet. His " eye in fine frenzy rolling " was lit with the flashes of genius that revealed the crater within. It used to be a pleasure to me to drop into his office in Cannon Street for a morning's chat. If I had any conceit about me regarding my own abilities ten minutes with Charles Swain would constrain me to turn round, and see if I had left a shadow behind me. For all that he was exceedingly modest. He did not seem to think that because he was a poet he ought to be worshipped, or that he ought to sit in state with a wreath of bays upon his head. He was content to move quietly, and unobtrusively among commercial men, and to perform the common duties of life after the manner of other citizens. He did not quarrel with the world, nor with fate ; and although he had a great soul he could see in little things that which gave him pleasure.

Swain did not often frequent the *Literary Club*, and he was seldom amongst us in any kind of gathering. But at his death we felt that something had been removed from our midst which left a vacancy that startled us by its magnitude. It was to commemorate that melancholy event, which occurred on the 22nd of September, 1874, that I penned the following lines—since published in *Songs and Ballads of Lancashire*:—

Another vacant chair ! another guest
  Hath left my threshold with his last " Good night !"
'Twas but an hour ago, ere yet the west
  Had lost the amber of its fading light,
One other friend departed, and he said—
" Good bye !" then sought his everlasting bed.

And gone before were others of the throng
  Who round my board at noon were full of thought
And feeling that found utterance in song.
  Th' Eternal Watchman's call the ear had caught ;
And autumn leaves around their footsteps fell,
As they, in tones that linger, sang " Farewell ! "

And there are others glancing towards the door,
  As though they saw a shadow on the stair,
With finger pointing to Heaven's glittering floor,
  And beck'ning to a festal gathering there.
These shall arise ere yet the night be gone,
And *one*—but which of us ?—be left alone.

He who last left the scene where none can stay,
  Woke with his touch the bosom's tenderest chord,
And sang with fervid lips that noblest lay—
  The love of man, and Glory of the Lord.
He " breathed of beauty, and eternal youth ; "
The " mind," its " grace, divinity, and truth."

And as he moved his fingers o'er the lyre,
  His eyes were ever streaming with a light
Caught from the glow of some celestial fire,
  Shining on worlds beyond the reach of night,
And grew the melody most sweet and clear,
When felt the hand the final touch was near.

As sings the nightingale when all is hushed,
    His song was never heard at noontide hour
Among the crowd of warblers; but when blushed
    The Night at Day's soft wooing, he his bower
Would seek, and from some solitary spray
Awake the echoes with his roundelay.

But never more shall voice of his be heard
    At our sublunar festivals, nor thought
Flash from his soul in glance as well as word.
    A spell upon his soul the angels wrought;
And whispering 'neath their pinions, "Brother, come,"
They bore the minstrel to his heav'nly home.

Say not you miss him from his chair to-night,
    Ye who have but another hour to stay,
But watch the flick'ring of the taper's light—
    A symbol of the close of Life's brief day—
And be ye ready, brethren, one and all,
That none may hurry at the Watchman's call.

Say—"Peace to the departed!"   He, ere now,
    Hath heard the songs we list for in our dreams,
But only faintly hear.   Around his brow
    The lustre of immortal glory beams,
In which the smiles of kindred spirits shine,
The scintillations of a light divine.

Oh, why this emptiness of human boasts—
    These songs in praise of perishable wine?
Our friend the guest is of the Host of Hosts,
    And sips the juice of an eternal vine.
The picture change.   The mourners are the dead,
Who wait our coming.   Which of us shall lead?

About this time a new weekly journal, published under the title
of *Country Words*, was launched.   It appeared to be sailing with a
fair wind at the commencement of the voyage; but the log must
have been misleading, as we discovered that after being afloat
seventeen weeks we had made no progress, and further voyaging
was given up.   The ship was scuttled, and we returned to shore,
much the worse for our experience in the publishing line.   To this
venture I contributed "The Marlocks of Merriton," and the poetic
"Epistle to Edwin Waugh."   The latter was afterwards included
in one of Waugh's volumes.

Cast adrift for a time, I hit upon the expedient of writing stories, or sketches for a number of local newspapers, supplying the same matter to each. I was very successful in this venture. To eleven weekly papers I contributed week by week instalments of my best known work, with the exception of "Daisy Nook," "Ab-o'th'-Yate in London." This step led me to attempt a further advance. I would start a journal of my own. This was a bold undertaking in face of my knowledge of the failure of *Country Words*. I, however, commenced the journal in the April of 1869. Some of my literary associates called me an "April Fool" for my temerity. The success of my little venture was secured the first month of issue, as it enabled me to redeem all I had risked. The circulation of the fifth number attained the, to me, extraordinary figure of 13,000, without employing street boys to push it under the noses of the public. At the following Christmas I changed the form of the journal to its present one, still keeping it to a *monthly*, and to its original price of *twopence*.

The journal kept on in this way for several years, but I had a brother-in-law in London who was advertising manager to a firm of publishers. Suffering from ill-health, he had an idea that a return to his native air might suit him better than remaining where he was. We at once agreed upon a partnership. We took offices in Deansgate, and commenced business under the name of *Brierley and Firth*. The *Monthly* we changed to a *Weekly*. Business was progressing satisfactorily when the greatest calamity of my life befel me; I lost my only child, then in her nineteenth year. This was a blow that took me a long time to recover from—even if I have recovered yet, though it is nearly eleven years since the sad event occurred. Humorous writing was out of the question for some time, indeed, any kind of writing, as I felt as if I had nothing further to live for, and that the blow might be the means of prostrating my wife. The circulation of the journal went down for a time. My partner's health continued to decline, and we agreed to give up business. We disposed of the journal to Messrs. Abel Heywood and Son, who still own the property, although *bearing my name*. My brother-in-law returned to his old situation in London; but consumption had set in; and the same year that took away my daughter deprived me of as true a friend, and the country of as upright a man, as ever plodded his way through life. Both uncle and niece now lay side by side in the cemetery at Harpurhey. Thus my budding prospects were blighted, and I had to plant afresh. For a change I allowed myself to be pitchforked into the **Manchester** City Council, which position I held for a period of six years.

Before parting with the journal I had completed my story, "Cast upon the world." It is my favourite, if the father of a family is justified in being partial to any one of his offspring. The story is partly autobiographical, the principal character being a little lame and deformed boy to whom I have given the name of "Humpy Dick." I have shed more tears over sketching that character than my manhood dare own to. After an interval of some months, during which time I did scarcely anything, I commenced in the journal another serial story, "Under the Berries." I was getting over the first shock of my great loss. This finished, I recommenced my "Ab-o'th'-Yate papers," short sketchy things that as reproductions were both popular and profitable. These have been continued up to the present time.

The following tribute to my daughter's memory is from the pen of the late Charles Hadfield, and is included in his description of a day spent in the cemetery at Harpurhey. Others will be found in the "In Memoriam Poems," which I have thought fit to append to these sketches.

"Only a few days since I stood beside a grave to which I had been led by a companion, who knew it, ah! so well, where for a little space we remained hushed and uncovered as if it had been the quiet chapel of a cathedral. For some time we did not break the silence. Half way down the green slope, close to the park, the grave lies somewhat sequestered; all around was the poetry of trees, some of the foliage making pretty shadows on the headstone. The little birds were there with their cheerful chirrup, as if there was no sorrow in the world! The old lines recurred to memory—

'The little birds that tune their morning's joy,
Make her moans sad with their sweet melody.'

My friend and I parted soon, but returning alone at another time I read on a headstone of elegant design, and much quiet beauty, the following inscription—

IT CAME UP
LATE IN THE SPRING
AND BLOOMED AT HARVEST
TIME. THE REAPER WEPT AS
HE GATHERED THE SHORN FLOWER
AND BOUND IT WITH THE RIPENED
GRAIN, IN THE SHEAF OF THE ETERNAL.

IN LOVING MEMORY OF
ANNIE,
Daughter of Ben. and Esther Brierley,
Of Collyhurst,
Who departed this life June 18th, 1875.
Aged 18 years and 7 months.

Over the sacred dust below lay a pretty coverlid of old English wall-flower, starred with the immaculate whiteness—dazzling pure —of many daisies.

I suppose it has not entered into the heart of man or woman, who has not suffered in like manner, to realise the dumb and tear-less agony of bereavements such as these. 'Total eclipse!' Not wild lamentations, nor speechless pain, nor tears, nor wringing of hands, can express it. 'There is no sorrow like unto my sorrow.'

> ' He who hath bent him o'er the dead
> Ere the first day of death is fled,
> The first dark day of nothingness,
> The last of danger and distress,
> (Before Decay's effacing fingers
> Have swept the lines where beauty lingers),
> The rapture of repose that's there—
> The fixed yet tender rays that streak
> The langour of the placid cheek,
> And—but for that sad shrouded eye
> That fires not, wins not, weeps not, now.
> And but for that chill, changeless brow,
> Where cold obstruction's apathy
> Appals the gazing mourner's heart,
> As if to him it could impart
> The doom he dreads yet dwells upon.
> Yes, but for these and these alone,
> Some moments, ay, one treacherous hour,
> He still might doubt the tyrant's power,
> So fair, so calm, so softly sealed,
> The first last look by death revealed.
>
> .   .   .   .   .   .
>
> So coldly sweet, so deadly fair,
> We start, for a soul is wanting there.'

These exquisite lines of Byron, so marvellously touching, and stamped with a truth only revealed to the eye of genius, have yielded a sad consolation to many a broken-hearted English mourner.

I have already referred to the perennial spirit of Hope which environs our English burial grounds like an atmosphere of light. Deep down in every human bosom, there dwells an aspiration and a faith that whatever worldly dulness, or blindness, or waywardness of Fate, or mystery of Providence, may intervene, there is in the mysterious future a moment of thrice-blessed and ecstatic reunion when not Time nor Death can longer keep parent and child asunder. A living poet, in his latest lines, has perfectly expressed the feeling :—

> ' Never the time and place
>   And the loved one all together !
> This path—how soft to pace !
>   This day—what magic weather !
> Where is the loved one's face,
> In a dream that loved one's face meets mine,
> But the house is narrow, the place is bleak.
>
> .   .   .   .   .   .
>
> Do I hold the past,
> Thus firm and fast,
> Yet doubt if the future hold I can ?
> This path so soft to pace, shall lead
> Thro' the magic of May to herself indeed !
> Or narrow, if needs the house must be,
> Outside are the storms and the strangers : we.
> Oh, close, safe, warm sleep, I and she—
> ——I and she ! '

It is ordained that this dear daughter's grave is never to be disturbed. Lying close beside it is another grave on which a clear letterless stone slab is resting. This is the spot where, by-and-by, they will come to sleep beside their lost and only darling—they—the father and the mother, Ben and Esther Brierley ; then, when all tears are wiped away and there shall be no more sorrow. The death of young Annie Brierley was made especially pathetic by some of the circumstances connected with it. She was to have been the bridesmaid at her cousin's wedding. All the pretty dresses and laces and ornaments had been chosen for the joyous occasion. The festival was anticipated by the stricken girl with that kind of desperate delight which is born of hoping against hope.

She was suffering. A doubt would have been cruel, and it was not whispered. The bridesmaid was ready! Dressed in the beautiful wedding raiment prepared for her, and arrayed in all the dainty garniture becoming such a day of gladness, the beautiful girl was ready—as she lay white and dead in her coffin.

The story was so strange and pitiful that all the country side was saddened by it. Kind-hearted neighbours and pitying crowds mournfully pressed for leave to look upon a sight so fair and sad; and from long distances they came and came, and were not denied. And thus Ben's one ewe lamb, the little princess, lay in her coffin beautiful and in State, like a Pontiff or an Emperor, her eyes closed softly in a dream of happiness, and her pale lips, on which a faint smile lay like a flower, sealed with an everlasting silence! The scene will not be soon effaced from the memory of many a sobbing, pitying beholder."

It is possible the public had noticed a depreciation in the quality of my work. I felt it myself, and determined upon a second visit to America, in the hope that my mental vigour might be restored. Previous to my departure I addressed the following to my readers:—

" I have lived long enough to discover that continuous brain work for a quarter of a century does not carry with it the freshness and vigour of early effort. I am conscious of a rapid falling off of both. The pump works with uncertainty when the well is nearly dry; and it is with an idea of replenishing for a short time that I have determined upon revisiting America. In the western clime the atmosphere is lighter; and from its influence, thought flows more freely, and writing is less of a task. I am hoping it will enable me to write a book that will be a fitting termination to an arduous and chequered career, for such mine has been. Our readers will hear from me in a few days after my landing at New York; and I intend that the correspondence shall be continued weekly, during my stay on the other side of the Atlantic. I commend to them the memory of a life, which, although it may not have been spotless, has in the main been earnestly devoted to the welfare of the class from which I sprang. If I have left any 'footprints on the sands of time,' I hope they may be carefully preserved beyond the period when my pilgrimage shall have ended. By the time this note is in the reader's hand, I shall have seen the last of my native shore for a period of nearly six months (1884). When I return I hope to be sufficiently refreshed and invigorated to occasionally find something for a willing hand to do."

F

My long holiday, and the salubrious climate of America had their desired effect. I returned home a new man. It was previous to my setting out that a public testimonial was set on foot, to be presented to me on my return. My native townspeople entertained me at a " farewell " soiree, and presented me with a splendid album, containing twenty-seven photographic views of familiar places, as well as the portraits of a large number of friends and celebrities. The views were taken by Mr. Squire Knott, of Oldham. a task of much difficulty. I was feted in other places than Failsworth— Manchester, Oldham, Leigh, and Clayton Bridge. In Manchester a performance was given at the Prince's Theatre in aid of the " testimonial " fund, and the example was followed in Oldham. The testimonial was presented to me on the 17th of March in the following year. I append a report of the proceedings as given in the Manchester papers.

TESTIMONIAL TO MR. BEN BRIERLEY.

The testimonial which has been raised by public subscription was yesterday presented to Mr. Ben Brierley in the presence of a large number of his friends, who met together in the Mayor's Parlour of the Town Hall, in this city. The Mayor (Mr. Alderman Harwood) presided, and he was supported by gentlemen from Manchester and many of the surrounding towns. Among others present were Mr. F. R. Hollins, Mr. Samuel Barlow, the Mayor of Ashton (Mr. Alderman James Walker), Mr. H. M. Langley, Mr. J. H. Nodal, Mr. E. Walmsley (Stockport), Mr. J. F. Crosland, Mr. Charles Hardwick, Mr. George Milner, Mr. Samuel Broadbent (Mossley), Mr. G. Candelet, Mr. James Collins, Mr. S. P. Bidder, Mr. Harry Rawson, Mr. R. A. Armitage, Dr. Samuelson, Mr. W. E. A. Axon, Mr. W. P. Owen (Liverpool), Major Smith (Ashton-under-Lyne), Mr. J. Fletcher (Ashton), Mr. E. O. Bleakley, M. W. Telford Gunson, Mr. R. Dottie, Mr. Thomas Black, Mr. R. E. Johnson, Mr. W. H. Guest, Mr. L. Read, Mr. J. Swindells, Mr. E. Low, Mr. H. Berry, Mr. James Dronsfield, Mr. G. Woodruff, Mr. James Bridge, Mr. J. Richardson, Mr. W. Kershaw, Mr. Richard Timperley, Mr. Jos. Lockhart, Mr. M. Wolstenholme, Mr. James Burgess, Mr. J. Bradbury, Mr. J. Wilcock, Mr. J. Newton, Mr. J. Lawton, Mr. S. Buckley, Mr. P. Jackson, Mr. W. Hague, Mr. J. Stones, Mr. H. Nutter, and Mr. Alderman T. H. Jenkins. Letters of apology for absence were read from Mr. T. R. Wilkinson, Mr. A. Mellor, and Mr. Alderman Abel Heywood. Mr. Wilkinson, who was treasurer of the testimonial fund, in his letter stated that it might have been well if the amount of the. fund had reached a round £1,000, but Mr. Brierley would no doubt be gratified to know that a large part of the money obtained had been given in small sums, which testified to his popularity among the people.

Mr. Frank Hollins (hon. secretary of the fund) stated that the treasurer had a balance in hand of £663 2s. 1d., and there were promised subscriptions to the amount of £20 which had not yet been paid. In addition to these, he was informed that he had received £44 outside the fund. The delay which had occurred in making the presentation was to a large extent due to the removal from Manchester, and subsequent death of Mr. Tom Nash, who was instrumental in starting the fund.

Mr. John Fletcher said he and Mr. Brierley worked together as lads at hand-loom weaving, and when that business declined, Mr. Brierley, by assiduous study, fitted himself for a higher kind of employment, and now his literary productions gladdened many hearts, and afforded amusement to thousands. (Hear, hear.)

Mr. Geo. Milner said he was there to concur in that movement to Mr. Brierley's honour as president of the Manchester Literary Club, of which Mr. Brierley was a member and one of the original founders. (Hear, hear.) Mr. Brierley was one of the six persons, who some 21 or 22 years ago established that club, and every member of it would feel that himself and the club were being honoured by the honour that was being conferred upon Mr. Brierley. It was true Mr. Brierley was what was called a provincial writer, but he would like to know how much of the very finest literature of this country was not provincial; he would like to know how much of it had not been drawn from provincial sources. If he was told that Mr. Brierley took his illustrations and the materials of his works from the well-known localities, from places with which he was personally familiar, then he said all the better. Surely that was not a thing to be ashamed of. Let them take the case, for instance, of such a great writer as George Eliot. How much in her novels was there that was not provincial. She drew her inspirations from provincial sources, and Mr. Brierley had only done the same, and the greater honour it was to him that he had dealt with that with which he was personally familiar rather than with that which was distant from him. He sometimes heard it urged against such writing as that of Mr. Brierley's that it was in a dialect which was not common to the whole of this country, and it was not at all unusual to hear observations of a depreciatory nature with regard to the Lancashire dialect. He was never disposed to defend a corrupt and debased form of the Lancashire dialect—(hear hear) but the dialect in itself, written as it ought to be, and spoken as it still was in some of the far-off valleys of the county, was not a thing to be despised or to be ashamed of. (Hear, hear.) It was a dialect which drew its words from the most ancient English sources, it was a dialect that was full of words of great strength and beauty, and it was only those who knew the dialect thoroughly, and who had also some philological information, who were able to judge how very many of its words were to be found in our earliest and finest poetic writing. Therefore, Mr. Brierley need not be ashamed of having spoken in a tongue which was and is understood of the people to whom he addressed his words. More than 100 years ago the question of dialects was placed upon a different level to that it had previously occupied by the writings of Robert Burns. Mr. Brierley's dialect was as much to be honoured as was the dialect in which Burns wrote—(hear, hear), and Burns himself had sufficient justification for the use of the dialect, at any rate so long as there were persons who loved to hear their own speech in their vernacular tongue, and to see it written. Sir Walter Scott had said that no man ever lived whose life would not be worth the writing, and this was emphatically true of such a life as that of Mr. Brierley, and he hoped their friend, before it was too late, would give them an account of his life, with all its struggles, with all its privations, with all its successes, not under the guise of fiction, as he had already perhaps in great part given it, but directly from his own heart. (Hear.) Mr. Brierley, he had heard, was the son of a hand-loom weaver. He was taken away from school when six years of age, and after that the story was one with which many in Lancashire were quite familiar—it was one of hard struggle for education to be got somehow. He (Mr. Milner) had heard that before Mr. Brierley was seven years of age he had read through his bible, and he need not be ashamed of that. (Hear, hear.) English people might thank that old Book for the deep-seated and earnest morality that still characterised them —(hear, hear), and they might be thankful too to the Bible for having taught them how to speak and how to write better than any other single volume possibly could have done. He could not help thinking that some of the strength and some of the force of Mr. Brierley's writing had been gained from that source. Then Mr. Brierley passed on to the study of such writers as Shakespere, Shelley, Burns, Milton, and Keats. How strange a thing it was that a lad born under such conditions had such tastes, such predilections develop within him! What could it have been but native genius? Native genius it was, and it was that genius they desired that night to honour. (Applause.) Not only had Mr. Brierley written that which had amused and profited many of his fellow-townsmen and others who were familiar with his works, but he had always written on the side of right, as he had conceived it, of truth as he knew it, and of honest and honourable living. (Applause.) He would not speak of Mr. Brierley's humour and pathos, but he would rather dwell upon that characteristic he had just mentioned, and which, more than anything else, was to his honour. A verse written by Burns to John Lapraik was applicable to Mr. Brierley:—

> Gie me ae spark o' nature's fire,
> That's a' the learning I desire;
> Then, tho' I drudge thro' dub and mire,
>   At plough or cart,
> My muse tho' hamely in attire,
>   May touch the heart.

(Applause.) He desired to wish Mr. Brierley long life and health and happiness and enjoyment in connection with the gift they were about to make him. " Ab-o'-th'-Yate " was a household word in Lancashire, and he was sure that afternoon they would all heartily say " God bless Old Ab." (Applause.)

The Mayor then rose to present Mr. Brierley with a silk purse, shaped like an old stocking, and a cheque of £650. He said it seemed to him that Mr. Brierley and Burns were very much alike in one respect, for Burns said of his father—

> He bade me act an honest part,
>   Though I had ne'er a farthing,
> For man without a manly heart
>   Is never worth regarding.

It seemed to him that Mr. Brierley might very properly say the same of his father. He regarded that testimonial as being intended to encourage others to persevere in a life of industry and integrity in consecrating their talents to the advancement, amusement, and improvement of their fellow men, assured that whatever was done in that direction was never overlooked or lightly valued. He wished for Mr. Brierley every blessing, and that he might enjoy good health, and consecrate his remaining days to doing good to those who needed it. (Hear, hear.)

Mr. Brierley, having received the purse from the hands of the Mayor, was heartily applauded on rising to speak. He said: I am pleased in more senses than one that this meeting has taken place, because it has given me an opportunity of briefly telling the story of my literary life, which from the circumstances inseparable from my social position, must have been a chequered one. I will not bore you with an account of my early days, but come at once to the time when I took up the pen as a means of earning a living—

"When I essayed to breast the sea of ink,
Unmindful whether I should float, or sink."

It is about twenty-seven years since I commenced my literary labours, my first noticeable work being contributed to the *Manchester Spectator*, published by Mr. Abel Heywood. It was entitled "A Day Out." This sketch was afterwards done up in book form, a second edition, published by Mr. David Kelly, of Market Street, immediately following the first. I wrote a sequel to this brochure under the title of "Bunk Ho." Both had a good Lancashire reception. These, with some shorter sketches, which had appeared in the supplement of the *Manchester Weekly Times*, formed my first volume, published by Mr. John Heywood, with the title of "Daisy Nook Sketches." And now the troubles of authorship began. Notwithstanding the flattering notices this book received from the Manchester, and other Lancashire newspapers, the *Athenæum* gave it a fearful slating. It was not criticism, or even an attempt at criticism; but an attack of such severity that it was undoubtedly meant to crush me at once, and for ever. It would have had the desired effect had not the *Spectator*, and the *Saturday Review*, come to the rescue. Each of these papers could afford to devote three columns of a notice exceedingly favourable, whereas the *Athenæum* had satisfied itself when it had flung three "sticks" at my head. These encouraged me to take up the pen again. "Chronicles of Waverlow" was my next book. The *Athenæum* attacked me once more with even greater virulence than on the former occasion. There was only a few lines, but they showed strongly the animus of the writer, who appeared determined that I should not exist as an author. He alluded to my first volume, which he said had been "treated with the derision it so richly deserved." I was sent to perdition again, this time with a heavy stone on my breast. But the *Spectator* and the *Saturday Review* again stood my friends; and I could not for the life of me see how all three could be right. The Lancashire press I have always had with me. Being in London, engaged for a short time on some almanack work, I was received with open arms by the members of the "Savage Club." I was selected from amongst six candidates to write a serial story for a new venture—*Colman's Magazine*. I commenced in the pages of that journal "The Layrock of Langleyside." In consequence of some differences among the proprietors a third number did not appear. I finished the story on my return to Manchester, and offered the early chapters to Mr. Peacock, then editor of the *Manchester Weekly Times*. Mr. Peacock was afraid a serial story would not take; but on my engaging to conclude it in nine weeks it was accepted. I need not allude to its success any further than by stating that when the eighth week came I could not see how I could bring it up on the ninth. I named this to Mr. Peacock, and his reply was—"My dear fellow, go on as long as you like." I took the advice. The story was afterwards published in book form, with a frontispiece by Mr. Charles Potter. I sent a copy to the *Athenæum*, with what I must admit to be a rather saucy letter to the editor. This might have been an indiscreet act; but I did it in a fit of exasperation; and with the feeling that that journal had done its worst to me. Mr. Dixon wrote me by the return of post, complaining of the tone of my letter, and giving me his word that he had not seen the notices that I complained of. The issue of this correspondence was a very kindly recognition in the *Athenæum*; and I forgave the Wellington Street Slogger for the pair of black eyes he had given me before. I was now fairly launched on literary work. I wrote "Irkdale" for the *Manchester Weekly Times*, afterwards published in two volumes by Messrs. Tinsley Bros., London. This was succeeded in the same journal by "My Grandmother's Clockcase," "Red Windows Hall," "The Fratchingtons of Fratchingthorpe," and "Ab-o'th'-Yate on Times and Things." This latter work led me to adopt the quaint *nom-de-plume* by which I have since been known. A change in the staff of contributors to the *Manchester Weekly Times* led me to take an independent course. I wrote for eleven local papers my "Ab-o'th'-Yate in London," the most successful of all my works. Ambition led a number of gentlemen connected with the Manchester Literary Club to start a weekly publication, to which was given the name of "Country Words;" but this youth did not live till he was breeched. It deserved to succeed, however; and I have no doubt, from what has followed, that it would have succeeded, had its local character been asserted, and maintained. It just lived long enough to publish in its pages my "Marlocks of Merriton." Now fairly out of collar, I had the audacity to start a journal on my own account, a journal that for a period of sixteen years has borne my name. In its pages have

appeared such of my stories as " Out of Work," " Cast upon the
World," " Under the Berries," " Fishing for a Husband," " The
Cotters of Mossburn," a number of shorter stories, and most
of my " Ab-o'th'-Yate Papers." Such close application to work,
and for so long a time, which for want of a more liberal education
has always been an effort to me, has had the effect of pumping me
out. But perhaps it was for the best that I was not born under a
more favourable planet. I should not have been thrown amongst
scenes, and a class of character, that but for my presence would
have been lost to history, as no one else has attempted to
describe them. The handloom weavers of Lancashire are now a
people of the past. Thinking fresh scenes might give my wearied
hack a fresh impulse, I paid a short visit to America five years ago,
taking " Ab-o'th'-Yate " with me. I came back refreshed, but
not restored. My health giving way, I paid a second visit in the
summer of last year. This time I had a longer stay and a larger
experience. The results of the two trips are now before the public
in a volume of 320 pages. An extract from this work was published in the *Manchester Guardian* under the title of " How
Englishmen have risen in America," and was so well received by
the public that a gentleman connected with the American shipping
trade has asked my permission to reprint 50,000 copies, which I
regard as a tribute to the breadth and accuracy of the statements
it contained. When these things are summed up it will be seen
that my literary life has been a laborious one, and not altogether
free from the vicissitudes that track the footsteps of authors.
Without speaking of the quality of my work, I hope I shall not be
accused of boasting if I say I have covered more paper with local
matter than any other writer of my time. If all that I have
written could be put together in book form, it would extend to not
far short of twenty volumes. But there is a lot of it I hope never
to see again—" Pot-boilers," and sketches written upon events of
the hour. I feel now that the time is past when I could engage in
any important work. I am no longer capable of sustained effort,
and may exclaim with Byron—

> " What is writ, is writ,—
> Would it were worthier ! but I am not now
> That which I have been, and my visions flit
> Less palpably before me—and the glow
> Which in my spirit dwelt, is fluttering, faint, and low."

It will ever be a source of satisfaction to me to think that in all
that I have written I have striven to rescue the Lancashire

character from the erroneous conceptions of "Tim Bobbin." The Lancashire man is not necessarily a representative of clownishness. In matters where sound common sense is required he is capable of holding his own with the natives of any other county. Possibly he may go a little further than that. In my literary creations I have not marshalled a lot of dummies before the public. There is not one that is upholstered—not one in whose composition the presence of the least stuffing can be detected. They are men and women as I have known them in life—never been set up for angels, nor degraded by being posed as bigger fools than can be found elsewhere. These I leave as a legacy to my native county; it is the only one I can leave; and if conscientiousness be any recommendation, it may be accepted with every trust. Throughout my public career I have endeavoured to conduct myself as a moderately good member of society, avoiding those traits of Bohemianism which are supposed to be the attributes of men who assume an exceptional position in the world of letters. In my private life I have not, by any out-of-the-way mode of living, distinguished myself from my neighbours, who scarcely know that I am a literary man. It is perhaps fortunate for me that I have a wife who has sprung from the same rank as myself, and who from that circumstance has been trained in the knowledge of how to make two ends meet when they have been very far asunder. I believe that has been the greatest blessing which has attended me, and given me confidence in my journey through life. And now I come to a duty that I am at a loss to know how to discharge, that of thanking the gentlemen, and working-men as well, who have subscribed to this testimonial. I am afraid they will have to bear with me, and accept the will for the deed. And the gentlemen forming the committee who have had the management of the fund—how shall I thank them? That is another difficulty I have no means of overcoming with satisfaction to myself. And to that noble band of artists who have given their work for the benefit of one not belonging to them, but to a kindred profession, a great portion of my divided gratitude is due. This generous act tells me there is a sympathy in the arts that the study of human and external nature encourages. To you, one and all, gentlemen, my thanks have now been so far mortgaged that I am left without anything further to say. But you may rest assured that there is a sincerity in them that words cannot fittingly express. (Applause.)

The Mayor was thanked for his services on the proposition of

the MAYOR of ASHTON, seconded by Mr. S. BARLOW, and this con-
cluded the proceedings.

> "My task is done—my song hath ceased—my theme
>   Has died into an echo ; it is fit
> The spell should break of this protracted dream."

And now there remains but one word to say—Farewell !

IN MEMORIAM POEMS.

IN MEMORIAM.

ANNIE,

Only child of Ben. and Esther Brierley ;
Born November 7th, 1856.   Died June 13th, 1875.

We thought she was our own for yet awhile ;
    That we had earned her, by our love. of Heav'n,
To be a life's comfort, not a season's smile,
    Then tears for ever.   "'Tis to be forgiven,"
We deemed her mortal—not an angel sent
From out a mission host, on mercy bent.

We were beguiled by her sweet ways of love—
    The growth of her affections round two stems—
As if they were of her, and from above,
    We did not note that from her heart the gems
Of her devotion were bestrewn in show'rs
Where'er she went, and gathered like spring flowers.

And her last words (coherent)—"I have lived,
    And have not lived "—were full of earthly tone
And utterance.   They, too, our hearts deceived ;
    Nor were we mindful till, when left alone,
We heard the flutter of a dove-like wing,
And a sweet strain, such as the seraphs sing.

Then knew we she had come in mortal guise,
    To teach us love, and charity, and grace ;
With sun-gold in her hair, heaven in her eyes,
    And all that's holy in her preaching face.
The scales had fallen, and our vision then
Saw that an angel graced the homes of men.

LINES INSCRIBED TO BEN BRIERLEY,

AFTER READING THE " IN MEMORIAM " IN THE JOURNAL OF JUNE 19.

I who have known not love of wife or child,
  And still am somewhat in the world alone,
  May fail to ease a sorrow not mine own,
Or lift affection's burden undefiled.

For I deem parent love the purest thing
  Out of high heaven—the most unselfish far—
  The love that loves whate'er may hap to mar
Its human idol, and will closer cling.

If that frail image hath small hold on life ;
  If through the human tenement appear
  The shining lights of some diviner sphere,
And what is mortal is unfit for strife.

I am a stranger to thy hearth and home,
  I knew not one whom thou hast loved and lost—
  Oh, no ! not lost—but one who first has crost
The mystic boundary, whither all must roam.

But I have known *thee*, and that were enough,
  When we together in the lists have stood,
  And each upheld the shield of brotherhood,
And song's bright buckler has disarmed rebuffs.

And I would give the sympathy of song,
  And add my lonely tribute o'er that urn
  Where all thy immortelles of song will yearn
Throughout the future, whether brief or long.

And now the *only one* that God vouchsafed
  To grant thee charge of, through those anxious years,
  Has left thee, childless, in this vale of tears—
Think of an Angel, and be thou not chafed.

Think of another saintly Seraphim,
  Smooth-browed, clear-voiced, with sun-gold in her hair,
  Blue-eyed, and lovely light of heaven there,—
Another spotless, white-robed Cherubim.

But grieve not of thy loss, which is her gain ;
　　And thou hast yet one other at thy side,
Who mourneth with thee, over one that died,
Yet lives, in perfect peace, in God's domain.
JOHN L. OWEN.

Bowdon, June 20th, 1875.

———

LINES IN MEMORY OF
ANNIE,
The beloved and only child of Ben Brierley,
St. Oswald's Grove, Manchester,
Who departed this life June 13th, 1875.
In her 19th year.

Farewell ! thou loved one !　Fare thee well !
　　Until I once more thee embrace ;
Language can't utter, nor tongue tell,
　　How oft in vision I thee trace.
From early childhood up to death,
　　Thou wert my joy, my hope, my pride ;
Now thou art gone, each fleeting breath
　　Doth fondly wish thee at my side.
I miss thee in the morning hour,
　　And when I view thy vacant chair,
The tear-drops fall in pearly shower,
　　Whilst offering up my morning prayer.
I miss thee in the hours of day,
　　When thou would'st gambol by my side ;
Pleasantly passing time away,
　　I looked upon thee with much pride.
I miss thee in the evening,
　　When I arrive at my dear home ;
Thy voice was so enlivening,
　　It cheered my heart where'er I'd roam.
I miss thee in my daily walk,
　　When thou would'st my companion be ;
And listening to thy friendly talk,
　　No father then could happier be.
But now thou'rt gone, thy spirit's fled
　　To realms of bliss to us unknown ;
Thy voice to us for ever dead,
　　Chants now before thy Saviour's throne.

Oh ! could I view thee, as thou art ;
　And gaze on thy angelic face,
Twould satisfy this aching heart,
　Banish my grief, and joy take place.
God gave, and he has ta'en away—
　Make me submissive to his will ;
Let grief no more my bosom sway,
　But peace and joy my sorrows still.
Knowing, thou'rt at thy Heavenly Home,
　Under thy Heavenly Father's care,
Where sin and sorrow cannot roam ;
　May all thy kindred meet thee there !

WM. CHARLTON,
5, Frost Street, City Road, Hulme.

June 16th, 1875.

SHE IS NOT DEAD.

(INSCRIBED TO MRS. BRIERLEY.)

BY FANNY FORRESTER.

SHE is not dead, your lovely fragile blossom—
　Your winsome Annie, with the golden hair !
The blessed child that nestled on your bosom,
　Smiling away each earthly grief and care.
She lives ! she lives ! her Saviour's arms enfold her :
　Her head is pillowed on His sacred breast.
Oh, selfish eyes, that languish to behold her,
　How can ye weep, when she is wholly blest.

Shame ! shame ! to mourn when she has passed for ever
　From this dark wilderness of toil and woe !
Poor captive bird, that loved its prison never,
　Yet warbled on because *you* loved it so :
She was an angel; yet the deep love shining
　In your fond eyes made her young life most dear ;
She felt your heart-strings round her white wings twining
　And in sweet pity would have lingered here.

But the dear Saviour who so kindly sent her,
　To win your heart from all unholy things,
With loving hand—for He had only lent her—
　Loosened the fetters from her snowy wings.

'Neath the green turf her mortal form reposes,
  But sisters angels bore her soul away,
With the soft perfume of the fresh June roses,
  For your loved darling was as chaste as they.

Perhaps you severed from her sunny tresses
  One graceful curl, to treasure ever more
With the gay ribbons, and the pretty dresses,
  That, but to please your doting eyes, she wore.
Close her piano, for around it lingers
  Dim, tearful memories of the happy past ;
Let it be sacred ! 'twas an angel's fingers
  That woke its notes to heavenly music last.

She lives ! she lives ! in loveliness, excelling
  The fairest flowers that round her footsteps grew ;
Nor could we wish her from her Father's dwelling,
  Where she has gone to keep a place for you.
Yet do you yearn for one brief moment only,
  To feel her kisses on your tearful cheek ;
"Oh, love," you wail, " our hearth is dark and lonely,
  Your mother's heart is empty, cold, and bleak."

Ah, sister mine, we mourn our vacant places,
  Yet when most desolate we feel our lot,
Those we have lost with happy angel faces
  Look down upon us, though we see them not—
When by the fire-side you are sadly dreaming
  Like radiant stars above your sorrowing head,
Your darling's eyes all lovingly are beaming,
  Though pitying voices say that she is dead.

AT MY DAUGHTER'S GRAVE.

ON HER NINETEENTH BIRTHDAY.

By Ben Brierley.

November's chills hang in the sullen air,
  The earth is shrouded in funereal gloom ;
The trees around seem fretful, weird, and bare,
  As here I stand beside thy silent tomb,—
My daughter !—loved alike by sire and friend—
Thy Mother's idol, thus to thee I bend !

It seems an age since last I saw thy face,
   Smiling to make e'en death a loveliness ;
And as the scalding tears each other chase
   Down cheeks that ever must be flooded thus,
I feel 'twould be the prime reward of prayer,
To see the glory of thine eyes and hair.

Now cold's the hearth that once thy presence warmed ;
   Dark is the room of which thou wert the light ;
Silent the music which my soul hath charmed,
   When home, and wounded, from the world's stern fight.
Thy stool—thy chair—the couch—all vacant now—
Cry through the darkness—" Annie, where art thou ? "

Thy mother nightly lingers at the gate,
   To watch thy coming ; and as pale the lights,
She says—" How long—how very long—to wait !
   Such girls as she should not stay out at nights.
All her companions are in bed ere this,
And I'm still waiting for her ' good night ' kiss."

This day thou would'st have marked thy nineteenth year ;
   A day looked forward to long months ago ;
That should have brought to us, nor sigh, nor tear,
   But such sweet joy as only parents know.
Who could have dreamt, or felt the galling fear,
That thou would'st hold thy birthday revels here ?

A bridal wreath bedecks thy marble brow ;
   The robes* enwrap thy form that should have swept
The path which leads to where we plight the vow
   Of love eternal—broken oft, or kept.
If shades commingle 'round thy hallowed bed,
Then thou'lt beseem the bridals of the dead.

Ah, frenzied dreams—ah, visions wild and strange,
   That haunt for aye this wilderness of air !
If in the great, inevitable change;
   Thou, God, seeth fit to show Thy mercy where
Love's blossoms are by thousands largely shared,
This garden of *one* flow'r Thou might'st have spared.

* She was buried in full brides-maid's costume, intended to have been worn at the wedding of a cousin. The poor girl begged of her mother, a few days before she died, that she might be allowed to wear the dress on the wedding-day, if not able to attend the ceremony. The request was complied with ; it served for her shroud.

They who would tell me life is but a span
　　Know not affliction—not the loss of *thee.*
'Tis woe, laid heavy on the soul of man,
　　That makes of time a drear eternity.
Life's sunniest moments fly the swallow's flight,
But oh, how slowly creep the hours of night !

Great God ! whose Will it was to take away
　　The *only* lamb that nestled in our fold—
If through His tears who wept on Calvary
　　The dear one's face we may again behold ;
Oh, let thy messenger of love descend,
To give assurance such shall be the end !

My pray'r is heard, a voice from out the clouds
　　Proclaims in trumpet clangour to the dead—
" Arise ye, shake ye off your mortal shrouds,
　　And put on Heaven's eternal robes instead ! "
I feel the flutter of an angel's wing,
And hear Heaven's choir their sweet Hosannas sing.

The vision's past ; the gloom is thickening round,
　　The mists enwrap me with an icy fold.
But here my soul hath its best solace found,
　　And turned to summer warmth the wintry cold.
Thus, hoping, dear, thy face again to see,
I weave those *immortelles* of song to thee !

TO BEN BRIERLEY ; ON READING HIS POEM " AT MY DAUGHTER'S GRAVE."

Oh look not in the grave, my friend,
　　Your dear one is not there ;
The child you love has passed away
　　To realms more bright and fair.

Our Father pluck'd your floweret fair,
　　Your bonnie gentle dove,
He took her from the chilling blast
　　To dwell in His warm love.

Oh, it was hard for you to part,
　　To let your darling go ;
To loose your tender ling'ring clasp,
　　You loved your treasure so.

Yet still 'tis not as though she'd gone
    Away; in midnight gloom,
As though her star of life had set
    Within the silent tomb.

She is not dead, she liveth yet
    Another life than ours;
A higher, purer, sweeter life
    Developing her powers.

She lives, she lives, your beauteous child,
    Your Annie, pure and rare;
Soon, soon you'll see her earnest eyes,
    Her shimmering golden hair.

All bright and beautiful, she stands
    Amid the blood-bought throng,
Her harp was tuned, her lips were set,
    To sing the angels' song.

The home in which your darling dwells
    Is not so far away :
One single step, and you will meet
    In radiant, endless day.

She has attained the perfect rest;
    You are wandering on the wild :
E'en now she's waiting you at home—
    Your lov'd, your angel child.

Rochdale.

JENNIE HEYWOOD.

—————

LINES ADDRESSED TO BEN BRIERLEY, ON READING HIS "AT MY DAUGHTER'S GRAVE."

Dear Ben, why droops that brow,
  So proudly arched, ere now,
With ail-nought-look of manliness, erect and firm ?
  And those quick glancing eyes,
  What sorrow in them lies !
Hath some bright thought of pleasantry slid from thee in the germ ?

G

That manly face of thine
With gladness used to shine,
Emitting rays of happiness and beams of joy;
But now thy fitful smile
Hath lost its charm awhile,
And that sly vein of humour seems blent with some alloy.

What unkind touch hath wrought
The pensive turn of thought,
That holds in solemn dalliance thy gleesome heart?
Whence comes that broken sigh,
That whispered " by and bye?"—
If there's a wound we know not of, O, tell us of the smart!

What? saidst thou, " She is gone!"
Thine own, thine only one!
The dear, and priceless jewel of thy heart and home!
Thy " garden of one flower,"
Drench'd by unkindly shower!
The one sweet rose-bud faded, and thy days of sorrow come?

O, is she, is she gone,
And left ye, all alone,
Twin mourners o'er her " hallowed bed," and " vacant chair?"
Well, truly, it is hard,
That under earth's green sward
Should lie, in bridal robes arrayed, a form so young and fair.

Such bitter stroke of fate
Makes earth most desolate,
Wanting that " only lamb that nestled in the fold:"
O, Ben, I know the smart
That lingers in the heart,
When that which makes the wound is past, and many summers old.

Weep, stricken soul, thy fill,
And let thy grief distil,
Regardless of the world's unsympathising ken:
Thy righteous tears of love
Will rise, like dews, above
Yon blue o'er-arching canopy, where loved ones meet again.

The flowers may sweetly bloom
Around her silent tomb,
Pressed nightly by the angel feet that come and go;
The tender grass may wave
Above her hallowed grave,
Swayed, grief-like, gently, through the evening twilight to and fro.

Blest be that bed of clay,
Where thou dost watch and pray,
Easing thy shattered heart with thoughts that pierce the ground.
But, Ben, she is not there;
The rosebud of thy prayer,
Transplanted, blooms in other soil, with other things around.

Unstring the silent lute,
The voice that charmed is mute,
And motionless the hand that swept an earthly lyre!
Content thyself to know—
It is—it must be so—
That there was need of such as her in heav'n's holy choir.

Manchester, Dec. 10th, 1875.　　　　　　J. GEE,
　　　　　　　　　　　　　　　　Superintendent of Police.

A BENISON.

MAY peace, sweet peace, henceforth abide with thee
From early dawn to deep'ning eventide;
And, when in slumber's weird-like trance enthrall'd,
May fairest dreams a soothing calm impart.
The sun, with travel, wearied, seeks repose
Behind the gilded cloud-peaks of the west,
And softly pales before night's sombre shades,
Again to rise in brighter glory far,
And flood with golden light the eastern sky.
May'st thou thus rise, refreshed and brave, and true
To Nature's instinct—then thrice happy thou,
And those who share thy sweet and joyous smile.

　　　　　　　　　　　　　　　　CHAS. C. HALL.

ABEL HEYWOOD AND SON,
PRINTERS,
OLDHAM STREET, MANCHESTER.

BEN BRIERLEY'S WORKS.

Price 3/6 each, Cloth,

WITH FRONTISPIECE BY J. SHACKLETON.

VOL. I.—

❧ DAISY ✤ NOOK ✤ SKETCHES. ❧

Contains :—A Day Out—Bunk Ho—Annie Howard—A Strike Adventure—Easter Holidays—The Bride of Cherry-tree Cottage—A Lancashire Wakes—The Charity Sermon—A Race for Liberty—Th' Gravel Gate Flood—A Daisy Nook Wedding.

"Full of clever sketches of Lancashire scenes and characters. The writer's outward course is well written; the style full of beautiful rural descriptive scenes, such as the lanes of the country present to the eyes of all pedestrian ramblers. 'Kurnul Jackson's dowthur' is a well-drawn character, and whether real or ideal has many compeers among the young ladies of the county. Hobson's allusion to the fine trait in her character of paying for the schooling of the poor children in the village of Daisy Nook, we take as an allusion to show how wide-spread the regard for education has become throughout the county. In no county in England will be found so many young ladies of means giving their Sabbaths to Sunday School teaching, as in this. The Whitsuntide processions of Sunday Schools in Manchester and the surrounding towns, prove this beyond a doubt. The scene at 'Red Bill's,' where three or four originals meet together to rejoice over real 'gradely stingo,' at the fall of Sebastapol, is a true picture of the feelings and habits of the humble Lancashire working man. 'Owd Tum' and 'Rackey the cobbler,' are both well-drawn characters, such as may yet be found in out-of-the-way nooks of the county, but which are becoming very rare in the large towns—where the constant friction of mind against mind rubs off all the natural oddities of character."—*Preston Herald.*

VOL. II.—

❧ THE MARLOCKS OF MERRITON ; ❧

THE GALLITHUMPIANS ; & RED WINDOWS HALL.

"It might possibly be deemed *soft sawder* criticism were we to attribute to Mr. Brierley either the exquisite humour of Cervantes, or the graphic power of Dickens. We think, however, that we are but just in saying that he possesses what is better than either one or the other alone—a happy blending, in a moderate degree, of both. Keen in his appreciation of the ludicrous, and at the same time a close observer of

*

those subtle distinctions which give the *morale* to the various incidents which make up the 'little round of life,' Mr. Brierley is a skilful and vigorous painter of the 'habits and manners,' the 'faults and failings,' the 'quirks and fooleries,' and above all, of those higher sentiments of our nature which are indigenous to every locality, and of which no class can claim a monopoly, to be met with in such abundance in the humble society which he has chosen for the exercise of his illustrative pen."— *Oldham Times, Dec.* 29, 1860.

VOL. III.—

✤ CHRONICLES ✤ OF ✤ WAVERLOW. ✤

Contains :—The Huntsman's Funeral—Dragged up— The Battle of Langley Heights — The Old Thatched House—A Cure for Love—The Buck Hunter's Gala—The New Shirt—Trevor Hall— Renewing Old Love—A Bit o' Mint Cake.

"Its author is not a mere worshipper of dialect, or a slave to provincialisms. He allows the Lancashire toiler to speak in his own vernacular, because he cannot utter his thoughts or express his feelings in any other tongue ; but in every other respect he is an English writer. His diction, generally pure, simple, and forcible, is sometimes elegant, whilst his moral tone is such as will commend itself to all, irrespective of county boundaries or local peculiarities."—*Oldham Advertiser.*

VOL. IV.—

✤ TRADDLEPIN ✤ FOLD. ✤

Contains :—The New Borough—A Fight for Love— Little Dody's Christmas—Beginning the World.

"The author of this little history of a Lancashire courtship shows that the broad humour so characteristic of the county in the days of Tim Bobbin, can still find utterance in the present generation. Mr. Brierley, we believe, belongs to the class who, in the truest sense, earn their bread by the sweat of their brow, and is a thoroughly self-educated man ; yet he writes in a manner that is quite unexceptional, and with an evident perception of what is picturesque and dramatic, to an extent that goes far to confirm the truth of Dogberry's saying—" Reading and writing comes by nature." Here and there are touches of fine feeling scattered among the comic elements of the story, as we see the smile hovering amidst the tears of every-day life ; and now and then we come to glimpses of natural scenery worthy of a place in the artist's sketch-book· Verily, these working-men of Lancashire are puzzles to the psychologist." *Manchester Examiner and Times.*

VOL. V.—

✤ IRKDALE ; ✤

Or, The Odd House in the Hollow.

"The characters are drawn with an ease and simplicity quite Goldsmith-like. The work is a pleasant one to read, and we can recommend it to the attention of all lovers of Lancashire folks and Lancashire scenery. The price brings it within the reach of the poorest amongst us, and its contents will well repay all lovers of the pleasures and pastimes of unsophisticated Lancashire men."—*Preston Herald.*

VOL. VI.—

✤ OUT ✤ OF ✤ WORK; ✤

OUR OLD NOOK;

THE FRATCHINGTONS OF FRATCHINGTHORPE.

"The readers of the *Manchester Weekly Times* will be familiar with the name of Benjamin Brierley, and will be glad to meet with it on the title-page of this little volume, where they will find a renewal of that genial humour, and that honest, hearty sentiment, so characteristic of his pen."—*Manchester Examiner and Times.*

VOL. VII.—

✤ CAST ✤ UPON ✤ THE ✤ WORLD. ✤

The principal character in the Author's favourite story elicited the following poem from the pen of Mr. JAMES BOWKER, an eminent writer and critic :—

"HUMPY· DICK."

A lad deformed and ill and lame,
　Without what makes rich children nice ;
No beauty or high-sounding name—
　No music in his trembling voice—
But in his eyes a ray of light,
　And o'er his face a wondrous gleam
Of hope, as crystal clear and bright
　As sunshine in a lovely dream.

A lad whose thin, worn hands,
  Clasping his crutches, plainly say
That hunger, like a giant fiend, stands
  Within the door to bar the way,
And keeps from entering ruddy health ;
  But whose sweet look tells of supplies
Drawn from the stores of heavenly wealth,
  Angels unseen bring from the skies.

And when we hear him o'er the flags,
  Come shuffling on with measured pace,
We know that 'neath the fluttering rags,
  There beats a heart of noble race ;
For eyes of angels oft may see
  In limbs deformed and faces worn,
True gentle-men, from vices free
  Too oft of wealth and plenty born.

For heaven doth send us such as he
  To teach us that its highest gift
Is not in wealth or luxury,
  But in the hidden things which lift
The soul above the dross of earth,
  And fill the life with nameless grace,
Until the child of lowly birth
  Looks nobler than one of royal race.

To teach us that to crippled feet,
  The upward road is made less hard,
And that the hosts of angels greet
  Such weary pilgrims heavenward.
Therefore, when such do cross thy path,
  Do thou in loving deeds recall
The duty of the one that hath
  To comfort him that lacketh all.

VOL. VIII.—

✤ THE ✤ COTTERS ✤ OF ✤ MOSSBURN. ✤

"Some gentle touches of Lancashire life and humour in a class of people to which Adam Bede and Silas Marner have given a new and romantic interest."—*Manchester Guardian.*

VOL. IX.—

✤ AB-O'TH'-YATE IN YANKEE-LAND. ✤

The result of two trips to America.

Mrs. G. Linnæus Banks's Popular Novels.

With Frontispiece and Vignette.   Bound in cloth, 2s. 6d. each.
Fifth Edition.

The Manchester Man.

"Realism that reminds us of Defoe; has no little artistic merit; exceptional interest."—*Times.*

"Is well constructed; has a good deal of varied incident, remarkable vividness, and interesting; the very atmosphere of the time and locality."—*Saturday Review.*

Stung to the Quick.   A North Country Story.

"Well told; is exciting; has interest; touches of real life and character."—*Athenæum.*

Glory.   A Wiltshire Story.

"Full of character, well contrasted, and well maintained.—It is deserving of praise."—*British Quarterly Review.*

Caleb Booth's Clerk.   A Lancashire Story.

"It is written with power, and is a capital story."—*Spectator.*

Wooers and Winners, or Under the Scars.   A Yorkshire Story.

"Must be recommended as an excellent novel to all who care for manlier food than that wherewith novelists commonly supply them."—*Graphic.*

More than Coronets.

"An exceedingly well-written story."—*Birmingham Daily Gazette.*
"Almost fascinating."—*Western Daily Mercury.*

Through the Night: Tales of Shades and Shadows.

"To describe what goes on 'Through the Night,' would be to deprive the reader of the proper thrill; but let him read the stories for himself, and he will be rewarded."—*Manchester Guardian.*

The Watchmaker's Daughter, and other Stories.

"A collection of stories told with much power."—*Leeds Mercury*

Forbidden to Wed.

"The story abounds in incide   nd contains numerous character stories which are vividly delineated."—*Spectator.*

Sybilla, and other Stories.

"Mrs. Banks writes with fluency and animation; her vein of sentiment is pure and carnest."—*Athenæum.*

Manchester: Abel Heywood & Son, 56 & 58, Oldham Street.

www.ingramcontent.com/pod-product-compliance
Lightning Source LLC
LaVergne TN
LVHW081347060426

835508LV00017B/1451